in sickness and in health

DAVID HAWKINS, PhD,

with Tyson Hawkins, MD and Joshua Hawkins, MD

HARVEST HOUSE PUBLISHERS
EUGENE, OREGON

Cover photo © bass_nroll / Getty Images

Cover by John Hamilton Design

David Hawkins is represented by MacGregor Literary, Inc.

The material contained in this book is for informational purposes only and does not constitute medical advice. The content is not intended to be a substitute for professional medical advice, diagnosis, or treatment. Always seek the advice of a physician or other qualified health provider with any questions you may have regarding a medical or psychological condition.

In Sickness and in Health

Copyright © 2019 David Hawkins
Published by Harvest House Publishers
Eugene, Oregon 97408
www.harvesthousepublishers.com

ISBN 978-0-7369-7420-2 (pbk.)
ISBN 978-0-7369-7421-9 (eBook)

Library of Congress Cataloging-in-Publication Data

Names: Hawkins, David, 1951- author. | Hawkins, Tyson, author. | Hawkins,
   Joshua, author.
Title: Is your marriage making you sick? / Dr. David Hawkins with Tyson
   Hawkins, MD, Joshua Hawkins, MD.
Description: Eugene : Harvest House Publishers, [2018]
Identifiers: LCCN 2018017296 (print) | LCCN 2018018869 (ebook) | ISBN
   9780736974219 (ebook) | ISBN 9780736974202 (pbk.)
Subjects: LCSH: Marriage--Psychological aspects. | Stress management. |
   Emotions. | Mind and body.
Classification: LCC HQ734 (ebook) | LCC HQ734 .H39195 2018 (print) | DDC
   306.8101/9--dc23
LC record available at https://lccn.loc.gov/2018017296

Printed in the United States of America

18 19 20 21 22 23 24 25 26 27 / BP-RD / 10 9 8 7 6 5 4 3 2 1

CONTENTS

To Christie, Jacqueline, and Jordana,
our wonderful wives,
who support and encourage us every day
to do the work we do!

Introduction

Connie is a busy 37-year-old mother of three. Her husband is a corporate executive with a large global company, which affords her the opportunity to stay home and homeschool the children. She has been active in her local homeschool organization until recently, when constant fatigue began to take a toll on her emotions. She began questioning her ability to provide what the children needed from her as their teacher.

"They are bright and active," she said. "I've loved being able to homeschool them. But they tire me out, more than they should. I feel guilty that I'm not doing more for them. I did a great job when they were younger, but it has become increasingly difficult to keep up with the curriculum and the kids since my health began going downhill."

Connie hasn't felt well for more than three years, but she has plowed forward. She came to me seeking counsel after seeing professionals in many areas of medicine.

"I've been to the emergency room twice in the past month," she said. "I'm exhausted from not sleeping well, having constant headaches, and chronic pain. I've seen MDs, naturopaths, and even an acupuncturist," she said with exasperation. "I never feel well, and I know I'm letting my children and husband down. The doctors have not been much help, and after all the tests and all the appointments, nothing really clears up my problems. I *never* feel well."

This is a story I'm hearing with much greater frequency, so I've become more equipped to ask better questions. I ask more specifically about symptoms, women's journeys to find healing, and the profound discouragement and guilt they feel when answers aren't found.

"The medical doctors tend to want to prescribe drugs or refer me for more tests with another doctor. That's why I'm here. They've decided I need to consider this might all be in my head since they can't find anything specifically wrong with me. I've gone from being angry at them to being angry with myself. So now I blame myself and feel guilty for everything—from the way I'm schooling my children down to how I keep the house. I just want to know what's going on with me. I'm not making this up. I can barely make it through the day. Are the doctors right? I don't know what to believe."

"So what have you done to cope?" I asked.

"The only thing I know how to do. I've gone on a search, mostly on the Internet, looking for what might be wrong."

"And?"

"Well, the only thing that comes up over and over is stress. I am so embarrassed. Is it just stress? Who doesn't have stress in their lives?" she asked.

"Tell me a little about where you think you experience stress," I prompted.

Connie went on to tell me about her husband, Charles, and his constant criticism of her.

"Nothing is good enough for him," she said. "He runs our home like an extension of his job. He's a bulldog. He always justifies his actions, blaming the kids and me for everything. He's never wrong. He's never satisfied. I find myself falling out of love with him and feel incredibly guilty about that." She paused, then quietly added, "Oh, my gosh, I think my marriage is killing me."

Stress Is the Real Story

How could her marriage be killing her? This had to be hyperbole. I must admit that at first I wondered about women like Connie. Stress is stress, after all. I've had a ton of stress in my life and never gotten sick from it. My sons, who cowrote this book with me, have experienced more stress in medical school and residencies than the average person, and they've never gotten sick.

How could her marriage be killing her?

The answer really does lie in the simple word: *Stress*. But how can this be? Because we all handle stress differently. While some handle stress by eating too much, drinking too much, or escaping into paperback novels, others get physically sick. Some thrive on stress—stress they can manage—while others become debilitated by it.

But make no mistake. Stress *can* kill us. Stress can elevate our blood pressure to dangerous levels. Stress can create anxiety, as it has in my life, or can cause us to be aggravated and irritated. Stress hides in many different places, behind many facades. Just because it appears as if someone is handling the pressures of life, it doesn't necessarily mean they are.

Stress has been called a silent killer. Perhaps you've heard that. But how is that possible? Stress is just a normal part of everyday life, right?

Yes and no.

Stress can be as simple as being late for a lunch date, or it can be massive and chronic from living in an abusive marriage. It can be fleeting and pass as quickly as it came, or it can linger with unending and horrifyingly destructive abuse. When stress hormones get out of whack, signaling the brain there is lurking danger, we either change our world and cope effectively, or as is the case of many reading this book, experience debilitating health problems.

So what is the bottom line? The bottom line is that stress can kill. It kills by negatively affecting our autoimmune systems, possibly leading to cancer. It kills by leading to atherosclerosis, which in turn could possibly lead to a heart attack. It kills by being linked to trauma, which leads to major depressive and anxiety disorders, leading to a loss of happiness and quality of life. It kills by attacking our heart and soul—the very core of our being.

This book will show you beyond a shadow of a doubt that stress can be simple or complex, easily remedied or, more often, very hard to treat. Either way, please read on and journey with me to discover more about that stress that kills your heart and soul—your marriage and your self.

Imagine

Imagine a time recently when you felt ill. Perhaps a bad cold or the flu had gotten you down. You were really sick. You couldn't work or focus on anything but how bad you felt. Canceling your appointments, you went to bed, hoping to recuperate quickly.

Fortunately you knew this illness would likely last only a few days. You reassured your employer you would be back soon. You told your family to make do without you. Buying yourself a bit of time, you pulled the covers over your head and slept.

Now imagine the same scenario, absent one thing: Hope for improvement.

What if this same sick feeling consumed you, along with a sense of dread that this was how you could anticipate functioning going forward? You would naturally feel dread for each new day, which would be sure to be the same or worse than the last. Mustering up the stamina to perform household duties and job responsibilities, you would slip steadily into a serious emotional valley.

Such is the world of countless women whose health and well-being have become severely compromised because of relational stress. It is hard for me to imagine. I complain when hit with the common cold or my allergies act up. It is hard for me to comprehend chronic stress and the physical and psychological effects from it.

Much has been written about stress. We know how debilitating it is. We know that stress literally wreaks havoc on the body. But chronic stress, the kind that comes from abusive relationships, does more than that; it tears down both the body and the mind. It shatters the foundation of living we take for granted: Emotional and physical well-being.

This book is the product of a horrific phenomenon occurring all around us, yet is rarely mentioned: The physical consequences of ongoing relational stress. It's about the physical and psychological impact of chronic, complex stress, or unrelenting stress with little hope in sight.

I have been practicing as a clinical psychologist for more than 30 years, and over the last few years I began specializing in narcissism, emotional abuse, and trauma and their stressful impact on marriage and relationships. The more work I did in this area, the more I noticed patterns and became more effective in intervening in these destructive processes. I watched hundreds of couples interact, paying ever more attention to the power and control tactics many men used to defend themselves against slights and perceived offenses. I have written extensively on these topics, leading to my last book, *When Loving Him Is Hurting You: Hope and Healing for Victims of Narcissistic and Emotional Abuse.*

In spite of my hyperfocus on the psychological impact of emotional abuse, however, I was absolutely neglecting a primary dimension of functioning: Our physical functioning. I simply was not trained to listen to people's physical complaints, not to mention the obvious impact of these physical complications on emotional functioning.

What began as a whisper turned into a scream in my clinical practice. A seemingly accidental observation turned into something I could not ignore. I began to listen with different ears, hearing what was not being said as much as what was said. I began to ask questions like, "Are you having any physical problems in addition to your emotional and relationship concerns?" The answer was a resounding, "Yes," leading to an outpouring of complaints.

Searching for Answers

The more questions I asked about stress and marriage, the more people shared. The more care and compassion I showed, the more they opened up to me. The old adage, "People don't care how much you know until they know how much you care," seemed imminently true.

What was going on here? What was I going to do about it? I wanted to talk to someone about my exciting "discoveries." It is unusual for me to talk to my sons, both physicians, about my work, other than in generalities. They have long teased me about being in a "soft science" as opposed to their rigorous medical school experience.

My first opportunity to bring up my findings was with Tyson, my younger son, an internist. On a Saturday afternoon during a round of golf I posed the question,

"When you're seeing a new patient, do you ask about what is happening in their life?"

His response surprised me.

"Of course I want to know what is happening in their life," he answered. "A buddy at work and I have started looking at the impact of trauma on patients and their tendencies toward addictions. We're using the Adverse Childhood Experience Questionnaire. We see a lot of patients who have very stressful lives coming to us for all kinds of problems. Why?"

I couldn't believe my ears. Here was my MD son sounding like a psychologist.

"Well," I said, "I've begun noticing how so many women having severe marriage and relationship problems are suffering from auto-immune disorders, headaches, sleep problems, and much worse. What do you think about that?"

"I see it all the time," he said. "I think a good doctor has got to stop and ask questions about a patient's life and how they are dealing with stress. There is absolutely a connection between physical well-being or sickness and emotional functioning."

This was an exciting experience for me professionally as well as a new connection with my son. We continued the conversation well into the afternoon. Both of us were pleased we had much more in common than we originally thought.

We ended our afternoon of golf with Tyson soundly beating me again, but with a profound sense of connection. His patients were my patients, and my patients his. We could see more clearly the mind-body connection and an overlap in our professions. With soft science meeting hard science, we agreed to carry on the conversation past this initial discussion.

Shortly after my golf date with Tyson I decided to ask the same questions of my older son, Joshua, a surgeon. I hadn't anticipated what he had to say on the topic.

"Well, Dad, I don't really know," he said cautiously. "I do know that when I'm evaluating a patient preparing for surgery, there's no question some are more emotionally stable and ready than others. I also notice that there is a huge difference in how patients respond to surgery and follow-up care."

"What do you mean, son?" I asked.

He took some time to consider.

"I don't know exactly," he said. "Some patients seem emotionally balanced and equipped for surgery. Others seem to be more emotionally distraught and tentative, even preoccupied. There are many who have a lot of complicating factors impacting their surgery and their recovery from surgery. Surgeons are just beginning to ask more questions and explore emotional functioning of the patients before doing a procedure. We're not trained in that and need to learn a lot more."

While more tentative than Tyson, he offered another perspective worth considering. Surgery is a critical life event that is affected by a background of critical life events. Many patients were initially seen by the internist and end up with the surgeon on the operating table. At some point these patients may be seen, or should be seen, by a psychologist or therapist in the consulting room.

This brings me full circle.

My sons and I are asking more questions than we are answering. We are considering what is already known about consistent stress and trauma and its impact on the body.

In Sickness and in Health is a groundbreaking book, a collaboration between individuals and their various helpers. It is an exploration of the impact of stress and trauma, what is already known and what is yet to be known about the impact of relationship stress on health and well-being.

I, along with my sons, Joshua the surgeon and Tyson the internist, who will share throughout the book, invite you into this new conversation.

One

THE MIND-BODY CONNECTION

*The mind and body are not separate units, but
one integrated system. How we act and what we
think, eat, and feel are all related to our health.*

BERNIE SIEGEL

How is it possible that I have counseled thousands of individuals and couples over the past 30 years and never asked how they were feeling physically? How could I be so naive and even complacent about the impact of emotions on their bodies? Why would I respond only if they brought up the topic, which they rarely did? I have spent hours talking to individuals and couples, taking extensive histories of their presenting problems, and yet virtually ignored the key aspect of their functioning—their bodies.

I prided myself in my thorough examination of their emotional history. I learned how they processed their feelings, how they communicated, and even the ways they dealt with conflict. I studied the impact of trauma on them emotionally yet was naive enough to consider their physical functioning irrelevant. I was after the specifics of their emotions, their joys and sorrows.

I considered the mind and body to be separate—kind of an East Coast–West Coast mentality, each considering the other to exist theoretically, but not practically. Mind and body were separate, having little impact one to the other.

While this may seem incredible, add to this fact that many people coming for counseling do not readily volunteer information about their physical health, perhaps convinced, as I was, that there should remain a great divide between body and mind. Most, it seemed, felt some combination of embarrassment, shame, and confusion and were reluctant to share all that was happening with them physically.

I come to this mind-body separateness innocently enough. I have always considered myself to be a practitioner of the mind while my sons, Dr. Joshua Hawkins, a surgeon, and Dr. Tyson Hawkins, an internist, were clearly focused on the body.

However much we have teased each other over the years, clearly, I have been far behind the times and I am long overdue to catch up. Longstanding evidence shows our minds and bodies are not separate, but actually quite connected. How we think and feel emotionally influences how we feel physically and vice versa.

Sally

Sally was the first client to really penetrate my thick wall of denial about the importance of the mind-body connection. She came to me initially because of her pervasive anxiety surrounding her marital relationship. She was quick to share about her troubled marriage and slowly, as she trusted me more, began to share more about her sleep problems, heart palpitations, and chronic pain.

Her severely depleted physical condition combined with her equally tragic relationship challenged my thinking about mind-body connections.

"Two years ago I was teaching school and living a full and robust life," she shared during our initial interview. She began to cry as she fumbled through her purse, pulling out a picture of herself.

"Look at this," she said. "That's me three years ago, 50 pounds lighter and a ton happier."

I couldn't hide my reaction, glancing from the picture to her face.

"It's okay to be shocked," she said, noticing my discomfort. "It's probably hard for you to imagine this, but I worked my way through college while raising two children and helping my husband, Jack, through engineering school. I was tired but still had energy to finish my teaching degree, start a career, and balance the demands of work and home life."

Sally was right. She appeared heavier than her picture and ten years older that her actual age of 36. It was hard to imagine her as a robust, active, and confident young woman.

"How have things changed?" I asked.

"I don't recognize my own life now," she said, her face strained and joyless. "I had to take a leave of absence from teaching. I can't get out of bed some days because of the pain. I'm a nervous wreck and have trouble sleeping. I can't think clearly. Am I making sense?"

"Yes," I said reassuringly. "What's going on?" I asked.

"I'm not sure I can even explain this," she said, fidgeting with her handkerchief. "The doctors don't have a clear diagnosis, but they are pretty sure I have some kind of autoimmune disorder. Maybe fibro-myalgia. I don't have enough energy to care for my kids, let alone hold down a teaching job."

Sally paused again as she fidgeted with the picture she had shown me. I noticed her becoming angry, shaking her head.

"This is all because of Jack. He's mean. I don't like my marriage and I hate my life. I feel terrible."

"Please share some more with me," I said.

"It's really complicated," she said, looking intently at me. "I'm afraid you won't believe me, and I don't know if I can explain it all."

Sharing a coherent story of their pain and suffering is hard for victims of emotional abuse and a troubled marriage. Sally was no exception.

"Jack and I fight all the time, and it's exhausting," she continued. "I've given up on him supporting me, and I have no friends left. I'm alone with my life."

What was Sally saying to me? How could a vibrant professional woman go through college, raise a family, help her husband with his engineering degree, and then fall apart? It didn't make sense.

"I'm truly sorry, Sally. Please share more with me," I said. I had to assure her I cared not only about her emotional well-being but also the phenomenal loss of her physical health.

"The past three or four years have been horrible, and I think the stress is literally killing me. My husband's anger and constant criticism and my unhappiness have taken a huge toll on my body. I've become angry too. I'm sure my bitterness is not helping my health. Doctors can't give any quick answers. I'm miserable. I think my body is keeping score and I'm losing."

I looked at Sally and wondered about the life she had lost. What had happened to her and why?

Initial Cynicism

I'll admit to initial cynicism. Sally's story seemed extreme. Was it possible that conflict—common in *all* marriages—was to blame for her being sick? Was her pain really that unbearable, or was it possible Sally was a hypochondriac, exaggerating her symptoms? Could marital stress really take such a huge toll on her body?

Sally smiled for the first time and thanked me for listening.

Hers was not the first story I'd heard like this, but it was the first I really listened to! Her story challenged my entrenched paradigm for viewing women with emotional issues and broke through my denial and cynicism. There had to be some real reason for her challenges— some phenomenal issues to cause a woman to go from vibrancy to disability.

Sally opened my mind to the possibility that something very troubling happened to women who were under severe, unrelenting stress. While I initially thought her story was exaggerated, I continue hearing strikingly similar stories. Troubled marriages, failing family connections, lost friendships, all taking their physical toll on countless women.

An increasing number of women calling for help with their marriages and other relationships were severely ill—some becoming agoraphobic or afraid to drive because of "brain fog." Some sought help from myriad practitioners, from medical doctors to naturopaths to osteopaths and chiropractors, desperate for relief for their debilitating anxiety and other symptoms.

Sally's story compelled me to think about things I hadn't connected before, but my skepticism didn't disappear overnight. My old filter of mind-body separation was hard to change. Psychologists and therapists treat the mind while physicians treat the body, right? I resisted the evidence that was mounting. I was tempted to dismiss Sally just as she dismissed herself.

"Most people don't really believe me, so I keep a lot to myself," she shared. "No one seems to get it. I don't tell my story anymore except to the rare doctor who will take me seriously. I don't tell my pastor who simply prays with me. I don't tell my friends because they tell me to leave Jack. I'm stuck."

Many Sallys

While Sally was the first to help me make the mind-body connection, hundreds have since come to me with similar complaints. One person is easy to question; hundreds cannot be doubted so easily. Sally and women like her represent a phenomenon that forms the foundation of this book—women struggling both physically and psychologically because of relationship stress.

I have now counseled many women like Sally who seek counseling experiencing vague physical symptoms from uncertain origins. These women challenge me to ask questions and seek the causes of their severe symptoms, which make them feel exhausted, depressed, and physically unwell. Initially I didn't want to be critical of their marriages or their mates. I didn't want to fault their churches or friendships. But the women, with their symptoms, kept coming to me with unanswered questions about their debilitating physical problems.

I was fighting an internal battle: Had I been overlooking something so critical for the entirety of my career? Were health practitioners, marriage counselors, and the clergy missing something, ultimately adding to their clients' distress? I needed answers.

Connecting the Dots

Finally, after so many similar stories, I connected the dots.

The connection, explanation, and hope lay in psychosomatic medicine: Mind-body connections where mental processes impact medical outcomes. This is not a new field of study, but I had never really explored the topic. It was time for that to change.

I began my journey to fully understand my clients' stress in their troubled marriages, families, and friend relationships. I wanted to fully understand the impact of relationship stress. Specifically, I explored the impact of severe stress on the body. I began researching post-traumatic stress disorder (PTSD) and complex post-traumatic stress disorder (C-PTSD) and the profound impact of stress and the flooding of cortisol (which prepares the body for a fight or flight response) on the body.

I couldn't ignore the symptoms these women brought to their counseling sessions. The immensity of their suffering deeply affected me. While I often couldn't *see* the impact, I began listening in new ways. I began asking questions that would reveal a profound new understanding of what was happening to these people.

Cynthia was the latest to contact me with some of the same symptoms as Sally. I approached her in a new way, ready to hear what I had previously ignored and denied. Now, armed with greater professional curiosity and compassion, I spent several hours asking all the questions I'm trained to ask. I explored childhood and early life traumas, adulthood, work, and marriage. Each dimension of her life offered rich discussion.

After some time, and with still a bit of trepidation, I asked the question I'm *not* well trained to ask:

"How are you feeling and functioning physically?"

Letting out a deep sigh, Cynthia said, "I don't feel well at all. I don't sleep well. I ache all over. I have frequent headaches. Sometimes my emotional pain *feels* physical and my physical pain *feels* emotional."

This was the moment I felt I got it.

"I think I understand, Cynthia," I said, "but I'm not sure what that means. I'd like to hear a lot more. Can you more fully explain what is happening to you physically and emotionally, and perhaps even give a few thoughts about what you imagine the connection to be?"

"It's really hard to explain," she said. "I can't even talk about it very clearly, so it may not make much sense to you. I feel sick when I think about the daily, ongoing stress of my marriage. When my husband walks in the door I panic. I wonder how he will make me feel crazy. I wonder how my head will spin. What I know for sure is that I will feel really stressed out, anxious, and then my body will react."

I encouraged her to continue sharing with me, though she began to tremble and cry.

"I'm so tired of all of this. I'm tired of trying to explain what is happening to me. My friends don't understand. My doctor tells me, 'You need to reduce your stress.' Finally I found a doctor who is running tests."

"Are your health problems getting worse?" I asked.

"Absolutely," Cynthia said. "I actually go to a holistic health practitioner and an MD. I don't feel well and have got to get to the bottom of things. I'm not sure anyone can really help me."

Cynthia clearly felt hopeless. Given platitudes and easy answers, she had been drifting from physician to physician, counselor to counselor, feeling worse and worse.

Cynthia is not alone. There are so many women experiencing similar symptoms—headaches, sleep problems, autoimmune disorders, brain fog, stomach issues, anxiety, and chronic pain. After they'd been dismissed as simply being under "stress" and needing to exercise, eat well, and get more sleep—all good ideas—I realized how much more medical and psychological attention they needed.

Let's look at life through Cynthia's eyes. She is unhappy and feels unwell. She suffers not only from her profound medical problems but from the emotional consequences of her unhappy life. She searches for help from anyone caring enough to get to the bottom of things. She has felt dismissed and disregarded time and again by medical practitioners trained to give quick solutions and medicine.

Cynthia and Sally are both suffering from trauma. They have been shortchanged. They have looked to counselors, physicians, pastors, and friends to help them, and at best they've received fragmented care. While perhaps they've received a listening ear, that was far too little real help.

Like most women I have spoken with, they suffer in silence. They fear talking to friends, family, or medical professionals about the covert emotional abuse occurring in their homes. They are tired of complaining. They don't even know how to begin verbalizing the secondary abuse they experience from people who minimize their pain, marginalizing their suffering. They are seen as hypochondriacs. Their pain worsens and their symptoms increase.

Cynthia and Sally long to feel grounded, in control of their lives. They long to think clearly, understanding what is happening to them and what path is needed to be healthy. They need support and encouragement. They need to believe their lives are manageable, healthy, and good.

Cynthia, Sally, and thousands like them feel none of that. They need wise, godly help, direction, and encouragement, which I intend to share in this book.

The Physical Side of Stress

You may wonder, *So what? How is this book any different from hundreds of others on the topic?* The difference is that we focus on how your relationships may be making you sick—literally—and what you can do about that. We delve into the origins of your pain, bridging the gap between medical and emotional, body and mind.

Psychosomatic disorders are usually physical symptoms that mask emotional distress. Perhaps preparing to see your physical symptoms as an expression of something else happening to you, such as problems in your relationships, will help you find healing in other ways.

Cynthia is part of a phenomenal number of women who are suffering both physically and psychologically. So many women are not coping well with the stress they experience in their marriage, on the job, and in their friendships.

Clare Kittredge, in her article "The Physical Side of Stress," shares that women are more deeply affected by the physical and emotional effects of stress than men. Women's reactions to stress are rooted in their body chemistry. Studies have concluded that 60 to 80 percent of visits to primary care physicians are for stress-related complaints. She reported that specific stress effects include:

- Eating disorders
- Stomach ailments
- Skin reactions
- Sleep problems
- Concentration difficulties
- Heart disease
- Lowered immune response[1]

Is there any question that the body will react adversely to stress? Clearly there is a profound connection, and prolonged stress is incredibly debilitating. Our bodies record and carry emotional distress, and they react with symptoms. Let's hear from my son, Dr. Tyson Hawkins, internist, about how relationship stress might present in the medical clinic.

From a Physician: Dr. Tyson Hawkins, Internist

There's no doubt in my mind that stress affects the body in very real, tangible ways. While less recognized and debated, emotional stress can actually *cause* physical symptoms.

That is not what I was taught in medical school, and I don't think it is what most of my patients believe. They come to me complaining of widespread pain, tingling, fatigue, memory loss, difficulty concentrating, nausea, vomiting, insomnia, and inability to lose weight. They are looking for a medical diagnosis and treatment.

Patients come to me after having sought help from multiple other sources, desperate for answers. They have often seen multiple providers for their complaints prior to me, where they left dissatisfied with the answers they received. Often, they arrive having read something online regarding possible diagnoses or have spoken to other people with similar complaints. Many have already formulated opinions about what might be wrong, ranging from occult infections (infections of unknown origins) to autoimmune disease.

My approach as a physician has always been to listen to their complaints and try to find the appropriate testing to clarify the hidden diagnosis and initiate treatment. Unfortunately, this approach leaves me, and probably my patients, disappointed. My first instinct is to doubt myself, questioning my clinical acumen. *There must be a diagnosis. Why am I not seeing it?* That is what I used to tell myself.

I remember the golf date with my dad when we discussed all the patients he was seeing with physical symptoms and significant relationship stress. He asked whether I had seen a similar association in my practice. The more we talked, the clearer it became that there was undoubtedly much more overlap between his field of study and mine than either of us had initially realized.

I have started to look at things a little differently. Growing evidence shows that trauma, be it physical, sexual, or emotional, can have severe and longstanding adverse health effects. This is well recognized in the condition post-traumatic stress disorder (PTSD), a condition where patients reexperience, not just remember, previous traumatic events with symptoms including flashbacks, nightmares, palpitations, sweaty palms, insomnia, elevated blood pressure, and even hallucinations. While PTSD is now well recognized, we should remember that was not always the case. It was only first described in returning Vietnam veterans, just 50 years ago.

The more I learn about trauma and its potential physical manifestations, the more I noticed it in many of my patients. Similar to my father, who had only been asking questions about his patients' mental health, I had been focusing on my patients' physical health. When I started asking more questions, I was surprised by what I heard.

Claire, a woman in her thirties, established care with me several years ago. She had just moved to my town of Bellingham with her husband and young son and was looking for a new medical provider. She came to me with the diagnosis of fibromyalgia and chronic pain. She was taking narcotics at fairly high doses. She did not work due to her condition. She had been diagnosed with anxiety and depression and was taking medicines for both. She did not look well when we first met.

Her most urgent need was to establish a relationship with a new doctor.

We worked together for several years running tests and adjusting medications with frequent follow-up visits before I finally decided to ask more about her home life. I had been dissatisfied (as I'm sure she was) with the results of various medications and interventions and was looking in a new direction. That was when she started to tell me about her controlling husband and how she felt trapped. In that moment a lightbulb went on. I think it did for her as well.

"I am not suggesting that emotional stress is the only thing causing your symptoms," I said. "That would be shortsighted. I would like to propose, however, that your emotional stress is potentially (and quite likely) making things worse. So, if you have pain, it will be worse if you are in an unhealthy relationship."

I paused to ensure she was understanding me. She nodded. I explained to her the likely relationship between emotional stress and what was happening in her body.

"Relationship stress impacts us. If you are worrying, troubled, and feeling stress, your body registers it all. If you don't sleep well to begin with, it will be more difficult, interrupted, and less refreshing. If you are feeling fatigued, it will be more severe, longer lasting, and life limiting. Everything is compounded, including healing, by relationship stress."

Claire seemed to understand and felt relieved after our conversation. Her situation is a prime example of what I am seeing in my practice, and what I believe my father is seeing in his. I want more for my patients than what pharmaceuticals alone can offer. It starts with asking the right questions and spending time in conversation.

The Mind Impacts the Body

It feels good to be in dialogue with my sons about these enormous problems and the mind-body connection. Perhaps "soft science" and "hard science" can now have a more in-depth conversation that will serve our patients.

Here I am, nearing the end of my career, partnering with my sons at the beginning of theirs. I've spent years studying psyches (the mind) while my sons have studied somas (the body).

It is a natural fit, however, since to some extent there is a mental aspect with every disease process. There are also profound physical effects from emotional problems. This brings us back to psychosomatic medicine, which I believe is the answer to many of our questions. Again, this is a field of medicine where a physical disease is thought to be caused by or made worse by mental factors. It should come as no surprise that the mind can cause physical symptoms. Consider that when we are frightened, for example, our body readies itself for trouble by increasing our heart rate and sending signals to the brain to release adrenaline into the bloodstream. When danger is perceived we may also experience nausea, shaking, sweating, and even heart palpitations.

According to Alex Lickerman, MD, in his article "Psychosomatic Symptoms," "The brain and the body are intimately intertwined, the brain sending out innumerable signals and instructions to the body every second, the body receiving them and sending back perhaps just as many...So the idea that an emotional disturbance could be translated into a physical symptom shouldn't be too surprising."[2]

How we think, and, specifically, how we view our world, greatly influences our degree of peace and satisfaction. Consider the individual who perceives her world as being out of control, perhaps even "crazy." Since her mind is in distress, her body records every distressing situation. Every thought registers a simultaneous reaction within the body.

Mind-Body Interaction

Beyond a mind-body connection, we experience mind-body interaction. A constant conversation takes place between the body and mind, and this conversation is powerful! Our bodies respond to the way we think, feel, and act.

Certainly, our emotions have a profound impact on our physical health. Every emotional reaction is felt within the body. This is, unfortunately, even more pronounced with distressing emotions. Confusion, for example, causes our brains to work overtime to understand what is happening to us. Anger causes our brains and bodies to shift into fight-or-flight mode, helpful in the short term but harmful over time.

Think about someone who causes you stress. Now reflect on your last conversation with them. Notice anything? Just the thought of this person is likely to cause a change within your body. Can you feel it? You likely have immediate elevated levels of cortisol and adrenaline pouring into your bloodstream. You experience increased blood flow to your major muscles. If you maintain this level of stress, you increase the amount of free radicals and inflammation in your bloodstream as well.

Now take a deep breath.

Imagine someone you care greatly about. Think about a special time with them. Notice where you are, what you are doing, and how you feel. Your brain is now producing dopamine and serotonin, the brain's natural version of morphine and heroin. Your brain will also produce oxytocin, the love hormone. Doesn't that feel good?

Additional Health Issues

In her article "9 Ways Stress Messes With Your Body," wellness editor Ashley Oerman notes that the biggest impact of stress in women is that it makes you exhausted. She notes that anxiety is often the culprit, keeping you up at night and triggering your brain to release cortisol into your bloodstream. The stress may be so frequent that your brain limits the cortisol it sends to your bloodstream, causing you to drag around and feel tired.[3]

As if the above issues are not concerning enough, stress has been shown to greatly impact the following areas for women:

- *Increased risk of heart disease and stroke.* Heart disease is the number one cause of death in women in the United States.

- *Hair loss.* Significant emotional stress can cause a physiological imbalance, leading to hair loss.

- *Poor digestion.* Prolonged stress can increase stomach acid, leading to irritable bowel syndrome and ulcers.

- *Depression.* Women are more than twice as likely to experience depression than men.

- *Irregular periods.* Stress alters the body's hormone balance, leading to missed periods.

- *Reduced sex drive.* Prolonged stress can lead to lowered libido. Elevated cortisol in the body also impacts sex drive.

- *Weight gain.* High levels of cortisol impact weight gain and decrease metabolism.

- *Insomnia.* Stress keeps us up at night.

Oerman adds these words: "Stress really sucks. It sucks up your energy, your desire to get to the gym, and even your libido. And while some stress can help you kick butt when your body goes into fight-or-flight mode, daily stress can mess with your mind and body."[4]

Women, Stress, and PTSD

This book was written for and about women experiencing relationship stress as well as physical distress. Chronic stress is the killer.

Stress is debilitating for anyone. But this book is about more than simple, daily-life stress. It is about the kind of relationship stress that kills the mind *and* the body. We are focusing on women for several reasons.

The majority of my referrals for counseling are women or couples in distress. Women, more frequently than men, ask for more information regarding stress. They are much more likely to seek videos, books, podcasts, and nearly anything that might help them understand their experience.

Additionally, many of my female clientele, and those treated by my sons, suffer from PTSD and complex PTSD, a debilitating anxiety disorder marked by feelings of hyperarousal, reliving the event and avoidance of that event. *All* of these women experience phenomenal stress, dis-ease, and often consequent physical turmoil.

In his article "PTSD and Physical Health," Dr. Matthew Tull says women with post-traumatic stress disorder "often experience a number of psychological difficulties such as depression, other anxiety disorders, and substance use-related problems; however, in addition to these psychological difficulties, individuals with PTSD may also be more likely to experience physical health problems."[5] Dr. Tull noted that PTSD puts women at risk for developing physical health problems because it puts tremendous physical and emotional strain on a person. The hyperarousal symptoms of PTSD put women in a constant state of stress and anxiety. These factors combine to put tremendous strain on a person's body, increasing the risk for physical health problems and illness.

Psychological issues cause both acute and long-term health problems. The extreme impact of psychological trauma, which can include severe marital stress, includes confusion, dissociation, panic, and agitation. Many who experience this will go on to develop post-traumatic stress disorder.

Finally, women often seek professional counseling when their marriages are crumbling because of emotional abuse, severe and protracted conflict, and other relationship problems. The majority of referrals for mental health issues stem from relationship stress.

Why Women Suffer

Connecting the dots, I've discovered women are more susceptible to relationship stress than men. Why is that?

Women are socialized to be the caretakers of the home, family, and even to a certain extent, friendships. Over 70 percent of married women with children under the age of 18 are employed outside the home and subsequently juggle their careers with family and home life. Women may value their work life, but they also greatly value their roles as mothers and wives.

Studies show that women suffer considerably more work-related stress, anxiety, and depression than men. Workplace sexism and family responsibilities provide additional pressure on women.

Certainly this seems to be true in my patients. Women are the ones who call for help with their marriages. Women are the ones who buy books on how to improve their marriages. Women are the ones who push for marriage counseling to heal dysfunction in their marriages.

Taking all of those responsibilities into consideration, women feel stressed out and struggle to take care of themselves. They often spend less of their time nurturing their own emotional and physical needs and fear being seen as selfish. Add to this the issue of hormonal balance associated with premenstrual, postpartum, and menopausal changes, which impact vulnerability to stress and depression.

A report by the American Psychological Association on gender and stress is particularly concerning. The report says, "Men and women report different reactions to stress, both physically and mentally. They attempt to manage stress in very different ways and also perceive their ability to do so—and the things that stand in their way—in markedly different ways."[6]

The evidence is clear: Women are suffering. Their stress is cumulative, and at some point they simply cannot tolerate any more of it. Women believe their stress increases over time from multiple sources, but relationship stress is at the top of their list. Women value connection and healthy relationships, and when these things suffer, women suffer.

The Path Forward

Mind-body connection. Cumulative stress. Relationship stress that becomes so debilitating that it leads to PTSD and complex PTSD. These are a few of the conclusions that propel us now further into the topic of how relationships can make you sick.

While we know much about psychosomatic medicine and how stress affects women, we want to definitively answer the question, Are your relationships making you sick, and if so, what can be done about it?

As we move forward in the book, we will also answer these questions:

- What is the real impact of relationship stress on women's health?

- How can counselors and physicians work more effectively to assist women in distress?

- How can we more effectively address underlying relationship stress?

- How can we be of greater help to women who are experiencing relationship difficulties and subsequent physical illness?

- Can better medical and psychological help be offered for these women?

- What more do we need to learn about the relationship stress and its effect on the body?

- Can the medical community better help these women?

In addition to exploring these questions, let's move forward now to explore specifically how an unhealthy marriage leads to an unhealthy body.

Two

Unhealthy Marriage, Unhealthy Body

I found him whom my soul loves.
Song of Solomon 3:4 ESV

For better or worse, richer or poorer, in sickness and in health."
We recognize those words, etched in our minds from the myriad weddings we've attended.

If you said them when you were married, not only do you know those words, but you believed them.

You had stars in your eyes, but your dream was not magical thinking—you had every right to believe your man would protect and celebrate you, for richer or poorer, in sickness and in health. You had every right to pin your hopes and dreams for your future on those wedding-day promises.

You had no inkling in that place of innocence that the sickness and health part would be integrally connected to your marriage. How could you possibly conceive that the person you selected to protect you would become the one contributing to your sickness? The fact that this is true for many women makes this book, and these stories, all the more remarkable.

Once we step back to get a wider perspective, reminding ourselves of the mind-body connection, believing our marriage has made us sick is not so far-fetched. Marriage is, after all, the ultimate mind-body connection.

The Ultimate Mind-Body Connection

In this mind-body connection, we're actually talking about two minds and two bodies. There is nothing in life like marriage.

In whatever culture you explore, marriage means two people sharing their lives in the most intimate way. This sharing of lives involves living together, sharing bodies, souls, and spirits in a physical, spiritual, mental, and emotional union.

Scripture is clear about the purpose of marriage and the powerful connection: "'At last!' the man exclaimed. 'This one is bone from my bone, and flesh from my flesh! She will be called "woman," because she was taken from "man."' This explains why a man leaves his father and mother and is joined to his wife, and the two are united into one" (Genesis 2:23-24 NLT).

What an image! Bone from my bone and flesh from my flesh! When I think about this image I catch a small glimpse of the heart of God. He had something very special in mind—this ultimate mind-body connection of two people, made as companions for one another.

Marriage is incredibly unique. It is the only place where one plus one equals one. It is the place where we let go of selfishness and lose ourselves. We merge with another physically, emotionally, and spiritually. This becoming one does not mean losing our individuality, but rather we feel completed, complemented to become far more than we could be as one person.

When considering this wondrous relationship, it is easier to understand how this ultimate mind-body connection could make you sick. If this connection has the capacity to help us transcend ourselves, it is also capable of causing emotional and physical pain. If this ultimate connection is unhealthy, if the person with whom you are so intimately connected is unwell, won't you also become unwell?

The Safety of Marriage

I have always appreciated the safety of marriage. There, in my union with Christie, I can be myself, warts and all. There I can come home, tired and worn, and still be accepted.

I have come to expect and rely upon this safety. I need a respite, as do you. My world is filled with the work I love, but it is also very challenging. I've chosen to specialize in working with couples who are often in crisis, experiencing significant emotional as well as physical pain.

On more than one occasion my wife has said, "I understand why you value peace, since your work life is filled with emotional tension. I understand your need to find comfort in our home and marriage at the end of your day."

Her observation is so true, and I value her validation.

Couples come to me in their most vulnerable and transparent state. Marriage is the place where we are real, where pretense is abandoned. It must be abandoned, for you simply cannot put on airs with someone you live with day in and day out. Your mate will quickly see behind the facade and confront you. Putting down your mask and being transparent brings safety with your mate. You can be yourself and be accepted.

Empty nesters now, Christie and I no longer hear the chatter of little voices or the patter of little hands and feet on the floors and walls. Our home is quiet and peaceful. We have chosen not to watch TV or listen to loud music, so the quiet is a respite for me. While I miss children, I also treasure our tranquillity.

Our home symbolically holds our marriage. We have crafted it to be exactly what we want and need at this stage of our lives: Safe, secure, and peaceful.

Kate

Kate initially refused to talk to me. She was fed up with counseling, having received little help from it.

Like many women struggling to make sense of her world, she had searched for information anywhere she could find it—YouTube videos, books, articles, and blogs. She had heard of me from watching my YouTube videos. She felt she had become something of an expert on the topic of abuse.

Though she didn't want to be involved in the counseling, she gave her husband the ultimatum to change or risk her leaving.

Kate's husband, Kurt, contacted me. He seemed anxious and withdrawn during our first session.

"All I know is my wife says she's done," he said. "Done! She says it's up to me. She says I'm a narcissist. She's done with counseling and says either I change and do the work or she's heading for divorce. I'm out of chances. I need to change."

"Is your wife willing to work on the marriage at all?" I asked.

"No," he said impatiently. "I'm telling you, she's done. She is really angry with me and fed up with all my promises—and I've made a bunch and kept very few. I probably deserve a divorce."

Kurt seemed to have hit rock bottom, where he was ready to change. He admitted to a long history of being defensive and emotionally abusive. He was able to clearly describe patterns of defensiveness, blame-shifting, and crazymaking, all terms he said his wife, Kate, had explained to him. He accepted he had made a mess of his marriage and wanted an opportunity to repair it. I agreed to work with him.

I shared with Kurt that I would need to talk to his wife to learn about his shadow side, the part of him causing so much damage. He sounded aware of some of his patterns, but I knew Kate would have a much deeper perspective. He suggested I e-mail her.

Responding to my e-mail, she agreed, reluctantly, to a phone conversation, but she emphasized she was tired of talking about their problems and had referred her husband to me for counseling. She was not looking for personal counseling, as she had a long history of seeking help for herself, but her e-mail filled in many blanks for me and helped me understand much about their relationship.

"It's his turn," she wrote. "I've done my work. I'm finished learning about why he does what he does. He needs to show me what he's willing to do. I'm sick from everything that's happened. I need to heal."

Her reluctance to enter counseling is not new; in fact, it's becoming a trend. Many women are tired of doing all the work to get their mates into counseling, only to have them quit prematurely or fail to fully participate in the therapy process. Kate was tired, angry, and sick.

Remember it was Kurt who made the initial phone call to me, but I needed to hear from Kate to effectively work with him.

"I'm tired," Kate began. "I've been working on this marriage for 20 years. I've read countless books on marriage, gone to numerous seminars, listened to podcasts, and done counseling. I'm sick of this stuff rolling around in my brain day and night. It's time for him to figure it out."

"Is he figuring it out?" I asked.

"Ha!" She laughed. "No. His crazymaking is still as crazy as ever. When I confront him, he flips it back on me. He gets mad, ridicules me, blames me. I'm not going to take any more of it. Instead of engaging in it, I just walk away. I'm not getting hooked anymore."

"Is that helping?" I asked.

"Is that helping?" she repeated. "I refuse to fight with him. I don't have a connection with him anymore, but at least we're not fighting like we have most of our marriage. He's realizing he can't hook me as easily anymore. It's sad because this is not how I wanted things to be for me and our family. Our kids are not seeing their parents in love with each other like they should. It's just sad."

I allowed her to sit with her sadness for a moment.

"So many women have worked long and hard on their marriages, only to be disappointed," I said. "Their work takes a huge toll on them, both emotionally and physically."

I decided to open the door, asking about the physical issues that nearly always accompany chronic emotional stress.

"Look," she said, becoming exasperated. "I need to get healthy. Do you understand? I have headaches, irritable bowel syndrome, and I've gained 50 pounds. I don't care if I look good for my husband. Our sex life is nonexistent. I'm tired, and I'm struggling to get my health back after years of being depressed, angry, and feeling hopeless. I'm really very close to being done."

"You've had to pull away from Kurt to begin to get healthy," I said.

"Absolutely," she said emphatically. "I haven't worked in years. I'm not ready to break up the family, but I'm preparing myself for it. Nothing is worth the price I'm paying. Nothing. I'm not putting anything more into this marriage until he does some work. Our two kids will be leaving for college in the next couple years, and I can hang on until then. I'll reevaluate when they're gone, but for now, staying away from him seems to be the best option. No more emotional quicksand for me."

I could hardly blame Kate. After years of emotional abuse she found a way to regain balance. She discovered a way to build an emotional cocoon, protecting her from the chaos she experienced when wrangling with her husband. The chaos had taken a huge toll on her. She had struck an agreement with herself—keep the family together and start healing. Give up the hope of a happy, healthy marriage.

If she was going to get healthy, it would be up to her. Her husband had proven he could not protect her. He had agreed to counseling, but whether it was too little, too late, was yet to be known.

Caught in a Web

Kate was caught in a terrible bind, and her body knew it. She was more than convincing when she told me she no longer wanted to work on her marriage. She had lost hope for anything ever being different.

In a fascinating article, "Thriving Despite a Difficult Marriage," based on their book by the same title, Michael and Chuck Misja candidly share what many Christians are afraid to say: Some marriages are simply troubled and may remain troubled.

> You're where you thought you'd never be. You thought if you did it the right way—you know, followed the rules and all that—your marriage was going to work, and you'd be happy. Happily ever after. Yeah, right. No one told you you'd be as miserable as you are. The marriage journey is tough, isn't it? You started well, but now you're living with a broken heart, feeling trapped in a difficult marriage without hope, and you don't even want to begin to think about the future. *What future?* Every morning you wake up in disbelief and every night you go to bed in despair. *Is this my marriage? Has it really come to this?*[1]

I applaud the Misjas for expressing the way marriage is for many couples. Like Kate, many are caught in an intricate web that is hard to understand and even harder to escape from. It's hard to understand why women stay in horrible circumstances. As you can see from Kate's story, the reasons are complex, and healing is a challenging endeavor.

You may have believed change should come easier for women in troubling marriages. You may have believed women should either tolerate bad behavior or be able to more easily change the relationship. Perhaps you've been tempted to believe anything is possible, that change is merely a prayer and positive belief away, only to find it isn't always the case. But now you see how difficult a troubled marriage can be, and your heart is filled with bitterness and defeat.

It is this mixture of hoping beyond hope combined with the sour taste of defeat that is so debilitating. The hope of change takes you to the bookstores, leads you to the Internet, and makes you seek out the best counselors you can find. The daily disappointments and craziness of your marriage keep you struggling to free yourself. While you never wanted to admit defeat, you're exhausted both emotionally and physically.

Exhaustion

It is hard to accurately describe the severity of the exhaustion that befalls the survivor of emotional abuse and a troubled marriage—the weariness women feel from the endless search for help, the bits of hope they find, and ultimately receiving little remedy.

When one has never been on a long, tiresome search for answers, one cannot relate to the exhaustion many women feel. Since you are reading this book, though, I assume you know the feeling of exhaustion. You understand the feeling of hopelessness.

If you're familiar with the 12-step program of Alcoholics Anonymous, you will recognize this imperative advice for those striving to recover: Never let yourself become too *Hungry, Angry, Lonely,* or *Tired* (HALT).

Those working through this recovery program know they must guard vigilantly against these symptoms, which often lead to relapse. They realize and live out what the rest of us know intuitively—being weary and lonely leads to making poor choices. We all know that when we're tired we are more prone to feeling discouraged, depressed, and even confused.

Exhaustion is no small matter and cannot be underestimated.

When our brains are tired from lack of sleep, too much worry, or, as in Kate's case, all of the above, your body stops functioning properly.

Dashed Expectations

We are always in the process of comparing where we are and how we are living with how we thought we would or should be living. The difference between expectations and reality is either hope or discouragement. We build our lives around our expectations. We make our plans, weave in our hopes and expectations, and move forward.

As I continued my conversation with Kate, her hesitation shifted and she seemed to want to talk about her situation. She became angrier the more she talked. Her sentiments about expectations echo those of so many others.

"I expected to be in such a different place," she said. "We built a successful business, have money and a lovely home. We have a strong church family and friends. We were facing a nice retirement. It could be perfect except for one thing—our marriage and the stress it has put on me. It's terrible. I can't stand it, and now my health has me worried."

"You had expectations for your marriage that didn't turn out," I said.

"Yes, and I hate it. I've worked so hard," she said. "I helped him make that business a success. I raised his kids. I helped build our nest egg—but have no real nest. In better times we were a good team. My husband is a genius when it comes to business. I thought we would have it all at this stage of the game. He's ruined our lives, and now it's up to him to fix it. It all makes me so angry."

"Tell me about the impact of your dashed expectations and how it has affected you both emotionally and physically," I said.

"We haven't done anything legal yet," Kate said, "but I'm sure thinking about it. I already feel emotionally divorced from him. Pulling away has been excruciating, but necessary. I think a lot about divorce. But because I feel like there's been a war taking place in my body, I can't make any decisions. My stomach is always in knots but all my doctor says is to reduce my stress."

As I listened to Kate I reflected again on God's expectation for marriage—two becoming one. Two people sharing lives together. Creating a family and living out the wonder and excitement of helping each other through life.

"I was raised to believe anything could be fixed through prayer and hard work," she added, "that there is always something you can do to turn a marriage around."

Kate paused.

"I still go to church," she said, "pretending everything is okay. No one in church sees what's going on, but my body and mind know the truth."

Magical Christians

In many ways Christians, claiming to be accepting and supportive, do women like Kate a disservice. Indeed, they can appear to be loving and accepting, but they are often unaccepting and even judgmental.

If you look closely you'll notice a strong undercurrent within the church that essentially says, "We will accept and support you as long as you do what we say you should do—as long as you follow the rules." There is little room for rebels, and any woman who leaves a man or even thinks about leaving a man for anything less than adultery is considered a rebel.

Kate is not a rebel. In fact, her adherence to rules and Christian protocol has kept her in an emotionally abusive marriage. Her strict faith keeps her in a marriage despite her body screaming to leave. She is a rule follower, but she is getting angrier and angrier about it.

Kate told no one how much emotional and physical pain she was in. She bought into the Christian culture that says we are to always believe in miracles, always pray for healing and change, and never doubt. She had conflicting thoughts of belief and hope versus reality and despair.

Now, don't get me wrong. I do believe we have a very big God. I do believe God cares for our every concern and desires to bless us. I don't believe, however, that God is like a big vending machine in the sky, that we plop quarters of belief into and, *presto!* Out comes our every wish. Not all prayers are answered in the way we expect them to be answered.

Kate, and women like her, fear opening up about their doubts and fears. They fear opening up about their troubled marriages, especially those replete with emotional abuse. They fear those who won't believe them, or worse, criticize them.

And so Kate keeps the conflict locked up. She goes through life accepting the expectations placed upon her by the Christian culture, her friends, and family. She understands no one really wants to hear about how miserable she is. She knows no one can fully appreciate her husband's incessant defensiveness and the impact this has on her and their marriage.

Kate suffers in silence, hoping for the days when she will be understood and truly helped.

Toxic Marriage

Clearly Kate is suffering and feels alone. She is in a toxic marriage—a marriage with detrimental qualities such as crazymaking and emotional abuse.

Much has been written in recent years about toxic relationships. Toxic relationships have a horrific impact on you. Why? Because they are toxic, poison. Like poisonous food or water, living in a toxic marriage will ultimately make you sick.

Psychologist Dr. Philip Zimbardo and counselor Rosemary K.M. Sword, in their article "Toxic Relationships," note five signs of a toxic relationship.

1. *It seems as though you can't do anything right.* The person constantly puts you down, criticizing you and forcing you to do things the way they want them done. You feel small and unimportant within the relationship.

2. *Everything is about them and never about you.* The person rarely asks about you and your life and is unable to have a two-sided conversation. They are focused on their life and what they are doing. You become smaller and smaller in this relationship.

3. *You find yourself unable to enjoy good moments with this person.* You dread facing the next day with them, always

anticipating conflict of some kind. Rather than having rare times of conflict, you discover there are more times of conflict than times of intimate connection.

4. *You're uncomfortable being yourself around this person.* You have begun to withdraw, living a false life. You hide your true self, your hopes, your dreams, and your wishes. You feel unsafe and guarded in their presence.

5. *You're not encouraged to grow and change.* You feel no freedom to grow, change, or express new ideas. You are relegated to the way this person has always seen you with no opportunity to be seen in a new and healthy light.[2]

Certainly Kate is living in a toxic marriage. She has long since given up dreaming with her husband. She is coping day by day. She cannot see far into the future, having lost hopes, dreams, and ideals for her life.

Good Marriage, Bad Marriage

If Kate's life is so dismal, why hasn't she left? Why does she cling tenaciously to her marriage?

Remember that her husband, Kurt, is finally seeking help from me. His last-ditch efforts don't mean much to Kate, but they do mean something. He insists he is ready to change. He seems genuinely sad and frightened about losing Kate and their marriage. Kate sees these sputtering efforts and has doubts about whether he might change. But he might.

Kurt is a mixed bag, though, and Kate knows it. He has promised to change before and has given only minimal effort. She overhears him quietly blame her to others, and then he scolds her for expecting too much. When angry he says she can never be satisfied. She gets hooked by his blame-shifting, keeping her feeling guilty about the possibility of leaving.

Let's also remember Kate has been married for 20-plus years. Most of her adult life has been spent with her husband. Together they created a successful business, built their dream home, raised two daughters, and are involved with their church. They knitted a life together, and it is nearly impossible for her to imagine a life without him, though this life is killing her.

This good-marriage–bad-marriage dichotomy creates confusion in her brain. (Our brains like predictability and steadiness.) This confusion causes stress and inhibits her ability to problem solve effectively. She doubts herself. Is she making up her pain? Could she have made up this toxicity? She's not sure, and her lack of clarity adds to the toxicity.

If life had been all bad, Kate might consider leaving more seriously. But her husband has some good traits. He is hardworking, has a good sense of humor, and is generally friendly. His schedule and finances allow for expensive family vacations, and these times are more tolerable for her, adding to her confusion.

Additionally, most of their friends would never believe Kate is miserable. They see the good side of Kurt and like him. He caters to this reputation, causing her to feel even more alone. She fears being seen as the rebellious one for not sticking it out with her husband. She wonders if her husband is right when he blames their marital issues on her.

Insecure, frightened, and confused, Kate finds starting over at her age a daunting prospect. She hears horror stories about dating after 50. She vacillates between seeing her marriage as tolerable and intolerable. Confused and weary, she has a hard time developing a clear plan. All of this, of course, impacts her physical health.

How do you think this plays out in the medical office?

From a Physician: Dr. Tyson Hawkins, Internist

There is no doubt that stress affects the body. It is generally accepted that stress increases your risk of medical conditions including heart disease, stroke, diabetes, and even cancer. It should therefore come as no surprise that chronic marital stress affects the body.

There are many theories about why this is. For example, many people can relate to being "stress eaters," overeating or eating comfort foods when feeling stressed. This can lead to measurable abnormalities in the body including obesity, high blood pressure, high cholesterol, and diabetes. These are all known risk factors for heart disease and stroke.

There are also many known hormonal effects of stress. These, however, are harder to measure. When under stress our bodies produce increased levels of the "stress hormone" cortisol, inflammatory markers, and cytokines. The measuring of inflammatory markers helps in detecting acute inflammation that might indicate specific diseases, and cytokines are proteins in the body sending signals and communicating between cells. They play a vital role in our immune system, regulating it up and down to effectively combat disease. Stress has also been shown to increase levels of cytokines called interleukins in a measurable way. It has been theorized that chronically elevated inflammatory markers and cytokines increase a patient's risk of plaque deposition in the arteries (hardening of the arteries), thereby increasing the patient's risk of cardiovascular disease.

Less well established is the effect stress can have on how we feel. Fatigue, pain, memory loss, irritability, and depression can all be physical manifestations of stress. They are harder to measure and not as easily recognized. They are not, however, any less important.

Fatigue is one of the most common complaints patients have when coming to the doctor's office. We know about many readily identifiable causes of fatigue, including vitamin deficiencies, anemia, thyroid dysfunction, and sleep apnea. A medical workup for common causes is often unrevealing, and that can be quite frustrating to both the patient and the physician. Chronic stress saps energy from our bodies and can leave us feeling drained. Mental stress requires energy. Think of all the time we spend worrying, planning, or arguing. It takes a toll on us.

Claire is a patient of mine who is on disability and doesn't work. Even though all medical tests have come back within normal limits, her fatigue is real. She struggles with chronic pain, fatigue, memory loss, and insomnia. She does not leave the house or socialize. It takes all she has just to get up and make it through her day.

For years she has undergone thorough medical evaluations looking for a unifying diagnosis for her symptoms. She is on numerous medications to treat her myriad symptoms. She has become quite isolated.

After thorough medical evaluations, she has been diagnosed with fibromyalgia, generalized anxiety disorder, depression, and PTSD. She has seen many doctors including a psychiatrist, rheumatologist, endocrinologist, and internal medicine doctor. She spends the majority of her time in doctors' offices. She is not happy.

She recently noticed, however, that she tends to feel much better when she is away from her husband. She has family elsewhere and visits them from time to time. While she is away, she is happier. She has more energy and gets out more. She sleeps better and feels her pain is better controlled. She is scared about the association she has discovered and is not sure what to do about it. She loves her husband but has not felt supported by him for years and is afraid to be alone. She does not want to give up on her marriage.

Although she's working with a counselor, she has a hard time keeping her appointments due to pain, fatigue, and lack of transportation. Even so, she readily admits that counseling has been beneficial for her, and she is very interested in more treatment. Her physical symptoms contribute to her isolation, however, which only seems to perpetuate the problem. Her husband resents the money she spends on counseling and frequent doctor visits, which only causes her to further isolate herself.

Claire's story is not unique. I meet many patients presenting debilitating physical symptoms who, when asked, admit to stressful and emotionally abusive home environments. Admitting to a stressful home environment is a challenge, and patients are not eager to do it. For my patients, making the connection between emotional stress and physical symptoms tends to be a struggle. It's often after many long conversations and thorough medical investigations that these connections are made.

Ending a Toxic Marriage

You can certainly see, from the perspective of a psychologist and physician, that a toxic marriage can be dangerous to both your emotional and physical well-being. Thankfully, if you are stuck in a toxic relationship, you do not have to stay stuck. Whatever you ultimately decide to do, you can begin a process of freeing yourself from toxicity. Let's explore some steps to begin the process of ending your toxic relationship.

1. *Admit the truth of your marriage.* As much as you may want to block the pain of your marriage from your mind, denial won't help. Change comes only after you face the truth of your situation. Take some time to reflect on, write out, and discuss with someone the true state of your marriage.

2. *Look at the ways you use denial.* For example, do you use magical thinking to tell yourself that everything will be fine? Do you promise yourself you will face the truth in the future, knowing the future will never come? Do you put all the responsibility for change onto your mate?

3. *Note the impact of the truths you discover.* As you write out and discuss the truth of your marriage, admit the impact of your marriage on your emotional and physical health. Do not sugarcoat your situation—that won't make anything easier.

4. *Let go of reasons to resist change.* Yes, there are ways and reasons to resist change. Change and growth are hard. We all know the feeling of staying in the rut we know rather than traveling a road we don't know. Be critical and reflective, acknowledging the legitimate reasons you might avoid taking an honest look at your situation.

5. *Heal your hidden shame.* Living in a toxic marriage impacts you. Enabling toxic behavior affects you and steals something from you. You are undoubtedly wounded and have suffered trauma within your marriage, perhaps even before being married. Admit this trauma and seek healing for your hidden shame.

The Mirror in the Marriage

Every marriage, no matter how toxic and dysfunctional or healthy, has something to teach us. Every relationship, in one form or another, can shed some light on our personality and give us an opportunity to grow.

Marriage can be, in fact, the best place to grow. Not always fun or easy, marriage challenges us. Perhaps no relationship is more contentious or challenging than marriage, yet marriage forces us to face our issues. We have an opportunity in marriage to learn how to relate in a healthy way, set boundaries, and discover new things about ourselves.

Scripture tells us, "Let the word of Christ richly dwell within you, with all wisdom teaching and admonishing one another with psalms and hymns and spiritual songs, singing with thankfulness in your hearts to God" (Colossians 3:16 NASB).

My marriage is no exception to the rule that marriage is a place for admonition. While free from trauma or abuse, I *am* married—and marriage, as anyone will tell you, is hard. Yet it is ordained by God to be a place for growth. It is actually the best place for growth.

My marriage has taught me, among other things, how selfish I can be. It has taught me that I want what I want when I want it, and I definitely don't like the word *no*! I don't like it when Christie points out my selfishness to me or notes when my immature behavior hurts her.

I've learned that my marriage works much better when I'm tolerant, forgiving, sensitive, and gracious. No matter what condition your marriage is in, consider it an opportunity for growth and positive change.

The Path Forward

Your marriage is probably the most intimate relationship in your life. It is the place you are likely the most vulnerable, exposing yourself to both the good and bad in the relationship.

While you may have found ways to insulate yourself, your body and mind record everything that is going on. Though you may have withdrawn, still you are affected both emotionally and physically.

What is the state of your marriage? It's time for a candid appraisal before you can really move forward. How are you doing emotionally and physically? I hope this chapter has given you an opportunity to step back, reflect, and consider your marriage.

Let's move forward now to explore specifically how you have lost parts of your life and how you can begin to regain them.

THREE

MY LONELY, DISAPPEARING LIFE

*Loneliness does not come from having no people
about one, but from being unable to communicate
the things that seem important to oneself.*

—CARL JUNG

At the top of Mount Bachelor the gnarled trees huddled together against the bitter cold. I had ridden this particular chairlift on many ski trips, but on this day I noticed how the trees hadn't grown. Weather-beaten and braced against the brutal wind, pelting rain, and blistering sun, the trees were barely alive.

The short, twisted trees told a story of adaptation. Though few in number, they were determined to live; they were surviving—not thriving, but accommodating their environment.

These trees were coping—adapting to their world.

In the field of psychology we often view coping and adaptation as a positive thing. We champion those who cope with hardship and survive, who accommodate troubling circumstances. I don't agree. The trees, like many humans under adverse conditions, weren't thriving, but were surviving by coping.

The trees remind me of women I've seen in recent years who cling to life, maintaining a modicum of calm in the face of a relationship storm. The women strive mightily to continue their careers, parent their children, care for their homes, and stabilize their marriages in the face of significant relationship stress.

But these women aren't thriving; they are barely surviving. They're just coping. And coping also has a powerful, adverse impact, destroying their zest for life and eroding their physical stability. Something is lost in the process of coping, and that is what this chapter is about—losing health, well-being, and quality of life in the face of ongoing stress.

The Process of Coping

We all face stressors. We find ways to cope, emotionally dealing with those stressors by eating, exercising, staying busy, shopping, or any number of other ways to ward off the anxiety of a stressful situation.

Coping is the process of using our conscious energies to deal with personal and interpersonal problems, mastering, minimizing, or tolerating stressors. We seek to minimize damage, turn off our emotions, and live as if nothing horrific is happening.

Coping is often considered a healthy aspect of life. We have all been taught to cope—to somehow move forward in the face of adversity. We may have been applauded for stuffing our feelings and plodding forward. But maybe we're taught wrong. Coping may actually lead to bad health.

We applaud those who cope with hardship: The loss of a loved one, an overbearing boss, multiple moves due to job circumstances, and even divorce. When a person seems to make it past a challenging event, we affirm them for striving to get past a stressful situation as if nothing has happened.

But something *has* happened! Damage has been done and is probably still occurring. You may be living with a troubling situation, where stressors insidiously mount. You cope with one situation, then another, and another. Soon you are living in a new normal, carrying tension and anxiety in your body. Coping, for its advantages, also exacts a toll, crippling you, much like those trees clinging tenuously to life at the top of Mount Bachelor.

Don't get me wrong. There *is* something laudable about coping with stress. We celebrate those who come through a hurricane and rebuild their lives. We sympathize with those who overcome severe illness. We encourage those who face an unwanted divorce, coming out the other side finding happiness again.

I've coped with each of these at times in my life. I braced myself for the inevitable job loss, coped my way through it, and came out the other side. I was the victim of a natural disaster and am considered a survivor. For the most part I framed the experience that way. But was that really true?

It all depends. Did I cope and survive, or did these experiences take more from me than I knew? While I stayed busy during these stressful events, I didn't spend as much time as I might have really dealing with what had happened. I coped, but the experience certainly took a toll on my emotional and physical health.

You may have read that our brains record everything that happens to us. While we may believe we are adapting and accommodating harsh circumstances, our brains may be recording something entirely different. Something like this:

This is a traumatic event. Hunker down. Survive. I'll help conserve energy and help you focus. This is likely a life-changing event. You may never be the same. The way you handle it will prepare you for what's coming next.

These are hard words, and they may cause you to stop and reflect on the price you pay for the stress in your life. Are you coping or thriving? Are you feeling your feelings, really living your life? Or do you believe your relationship stress is something you can cope with, as your body (and brain) record something entirely different. Even though you believe you can simply move forward with your life, your brain and body record your pain.

The Path of Coping

Elizabeth Kubler-Ross, who in 1969 wrote *On Death and Dying*, changed the way we look at stress and coping forever. She outlined what *should* happen when someone faces a terminal illness. Subsequent researchers and clinicians suggest her five stages of grief can be applied to both the largest and the smallest losses, including the impact of ongoing stress. She showed how stress could be dealt with effectively— or go terribly wrong.

Dr. Ross discovered that each stage must be experienced if we are to reach the other side of grief. Getting stuck means living like the trees on Mount Bachelor—coping, adapting, but not thriving. Living, but not living life abundantly. She believed we must go through these five stages if we are to be healthy.[1]

1. *Denial and isolation.* In this stage we tell ourselves that this loss is not happening. For our purposes, you might tell yourself that your relationship stress is not as severe as it seems.

2. *Anger.* Facing the reality of the loss you feel anger. Deflecting more vulnerable emotion, you may express anger at inanimate objects or other, safer people. You may resent the person causing you pain, but feel guilty about those feelings.

3. *Bargaining.* The normal reaction to feelings of helplessness and vulnerability is an attempt to regain control, trying to make a deal with the perpetrator of harm or even with God. You may still be trying to avoid facing the reality of the situation, an attempt to simply cope.

4. *Depression.* Sadness and regret dominate this stage of grieving. You may worry about the price and path of change. What can you do to end your overwhelming stress? You may begin to grieve the loss of your friendship or marriage, although you may not yet be ready to take the step of ending it.

5. *Acceptance.* If you allow yourself to embrace each of these stages, you will arrive at acceptance. You will face the truth and the truth will set you free.

It's easy to become "stuck" in any one of these stages. Coping becomes dysfunctional when we allow ourselves to face only partial truths about our situation, not fully embracing our grief and losses. We tell ourselves we are coping well, maintaining a stoic posture, refusing to cry, staying angry, or denying the severity of our circumstance. Facing our grief and the full impact of a situation, however, gives us a greater chance of making positive changes and avoiding the negative emotional and physical impact of coping poorly.

Cynthia

Cynthia was the perfect example of adaptation and coping. Separated from her husband, she now faced the end of her second marriage. She had remained in her troubled marriage for several hard years for many reasons.

"I'm only 38 years old, but I feel 60," she said, "and here I am single again. Two-time loser."

"Tell me what has happened in your marriage," I said.

"It is more like the story of what's happened my whole life," she said. "I've learned to cope with adverse circumstances ever since I was seven years old and my mom ran off with some man. I went to live with my dad, a series of stepmothers, and now I seem to be living out their lives. I feel so stupid."

"Why do you say that?" I asked.

"Look at my life," she said. "I'm going to be single again with two kids. I've tried to adapt to everything life has thrown at me, but I don't think I'm doing very well. I'm going to be living in a dumpy apartment now, driving a crummy car, and scraping to make ends meet. What does my future hold?"

I tried to think of something positive to say to her, though silently agreed with her. Her life ahead appeared challenging by anyone's standards. She was going to have a difficult time moving forward.

"I've got you stumped too, don't I," she said smiling. "My doctor doesn't know where all my physical pain is coming from and referred me to you."

"What is happening physically?" I asked.

"I don't know," she said, "and neither does he. He's giving me tests but can't explain why I'm so tired and weak. I ache all over. My whole body hurts. They don't know what's going on."

"The doctors can't tell you what is wrong?" I asked.

"Not really," she said. "They've been trying to rule out different possibilities. I don't hold out much hope. I'll deal with whatever it is."

"I suspect you do find ways to deal with adversity, Cynthia," I said. "There must be some lessons you've learned from your experiences."

"Yeah," she said firmly. "Be tough. Cope. Find ways to get through it all. Don't look back because there's nothing back there. Don't look too far ahead, though, because there may not be much out there either."

"Do you ever feel sad or anxious about your life?" I asked.

"I don't have anyone to talk to even if I did want to complain. I've always had to take care of myself. I don't have time for crying, and now I have to take care of my physical issues too."

"What do you mean?" I asked.

"I think my divorces, money problems, and relationship issues have caused incredible stress on my body. The doctors say that's why I'm in pain. What if I can't do this alone? What if my body completely breaks down?"

Cynthia wasn't really a tough woman, but by acting tough she'd been able to hold her fears and worries at bay. Now, though, I could sense that her physical pain frightened her. She had been through more hardship in her 38 years than most people experience in a lifetime. She may have reached her limits, this time because her body was screaming for relief.

Dissociation

Coping is, in many respects, a way to deny the full presence of something traumatic and to live *as if* life were normal. While Cynthia managed to act as if everything was okay, she was not really living and she was certainly not thriving.

Dr. Bessel van der Kolk says in his book *The Body Keeps the Score,* "Dissociation is the essence of trauma. The overwhelming experience is split off and fragmented, so that the emotions, sounds, images, thoughts, and physical sensations related to the trauma take on a life of their own...As long as the trauma is not resolved, the stress hormones that the body secretes to protect itself keep circulating, and the defensive movements and emotional responses keep getting replayed."[2]

What does this have to do with coping? Coping is a way of keeping trauma out of awareness. Cynthia avoids really "feeling and dealing" with all her past hurts and wounds and instead plows forward. She copes by dissociating herself from her painful past and present; her day-to-day events become less compelling. Van der Kolk adds, "Not being able to deeply take in what is going on around them makes it impossible to feel fully alive."[3]

Cynthia's physical pain may turn out to be her greatest gift. Perhaps her pain will awaken her to what is really happening in her life. Perhaps her physical pain will connect her to her body in a new way and awaken her mind to realities that require her attention. Her coping patterns have stopped her from feeling and subsequently from healing.

Refusing to Grieve

Cynthia's coping style was quite obvious: Suppress pain, be tough, and face head-on any challenges that come at you. This approach has worked to keep her alive, but not to really live. Though she had a life marked by disappointment, losses, and trauma, she didn't see herself as a victim. She denied and dissociated her pain and viewed herself as someone who coped well. That wasn't true.

Cynthia was not fully awake and alive. She was haunted by past trauma. It was clear from listening to Cynthia she carried a lot of anger and hurt. She had suffered alone with so much loss, and her life had become smaller because of it. She had never had anyone to listen and attend to her pain. She had learned early to push her pain away (which is impossible to really do!) and cope with life the best she could.

It has been said that "grief is the healing feeling." I believed that could be true for Cynthia. I asked her about grief.

"Grief?" she said sarcastically. "When I cried as a child, my dad threatened to give me something to cry about. I quickly learned not to cry."

"But do you ever grieve?" I asked.

"I don't know what you mean," she said. "I was pretty angry when I took the kids and left my husband. I was done with walking on eggshells, wondering when he would throw another fit. I was mad but I didn't cry."

"That's your way of coping, isn't it?" I said. "I do wonder if you have a lot of sadness inside."

"Of course I do," she said boldly. "But I'm not going to cry about it."

"But you may need to cry over your losses," I said.

"Maybe," she said.

Cynthia had made a pact with herself not to cry or complain—a pact many people make with themselves. Finally, after weeks of counseling and discussing her life, the incredible challenges of a traumatic childhood, and two failed marriages, she realized coping was not really living. Then, in a moment of vulnerability, she cried.

Creation of the False Self

Clinging to old patterns of coping, to our various attempts to not feel the full weight of our pain, separates us from our true self—the place we hold our true feelings and dreams for our life. We're all creatures of habit, and our brains like consistency, no matter how damaging this ultimately is to our emotional and physical well-being.

While coping may be a way to anesthetize our pain, we need to attend to our losses. It took time for Cynthia to allow herself to feel the pain of her losses and cry. She stifled her tears, clinging to the defenses she knew. She believed her narrow, predictable life might somehow help her avoid pain, which perhaps it did. But in the process she found her authentic self disappearing.

Cynthia was in pain—emotional and physical. Her body ached with worsening, diffuse pain. While her emotional pain had been relatively easy to disregard, her physical pain was not as easy to ignore. Was it possible that her emotional pain could lead her to both emotional and physical health? If so, this would be the opposite of simply coping!

Emotion is sometimes referred to as energy in motion. Our emotions inform us of what we need in our life. For example, loneliness informs us we are in need of friendship. Fear informs us we are in need of safety. Discouragement informs us of our need for encouragement. Emotion, felt and embraced, leads and guides us in making healthy, life-giving decisions.

While Cynthia had no one in her world to trust, we could say she didn't trust herself. Perhaps it would be better said she didn't trust her vulnerable, *real self*, which she kept safely tucked away. She didn't trust her feelings of sadness, hurt, and loss to lead and guide her. She would need to realize her physical pain was likely psychosomatic, and this would be her emotional work to do.

Cynthia's distrust of herself led her to creating a *false self.* She had left many parts of her real self behind, buried under much pain. She was living in her own shadow.

Patti Digh, in her book *Life Is a Verb,* says, "We get in our own way sometimes by not trusting that ineffable impulse...We ignore our own truths, the ones deep inside us, seeking affirmation outside instead. We cast our own shadows in that way."[4] After months of counseling, Cynthia finally cried. She was deeply sad. She cried for the person she had become—someone, in many ways, she had never wanted to become. She cried when she began to understand the armor she carried to protect her vulnerable self. She cried as she began to understand all she had lost.

I invited Cynthia on a journey I ask all my patients to take. This journey has simple instructions but follows a rugged path. I asked her to reflect on who she wished she had become. Who had she always secretly dreamed of being? If she could thrive, really grow, what might she do and who might she be? What might an authentic life be for her?

"I wanted to be a teacher," she said. "I love kids and always believed I could teach and inspire children. Now it's probably too late."

"Why?" I asked. "Our colleges are filled with thirty- and fortysomethings returning to school."

Cynthia's eyes lit up as she allowed herself to consider this.

Reflections of a Real Life

Becoming real means letting go of our false self and leaning into our real self. It always involves some degree of fear as we stretch into someone we may not fully know. It almost always involves feeling feelings we have suppressed, thinking thoughts we've pushed away, and considering possibilities. It can be an exciting and scary journey.

I asked Cynthia to reflect and dream about a life she might have lived had circumstances been more favorable. It was a difficult assignment, since her life was wrapped with so much familiarity. It's hard to dream of actually being someone different than we are.

I asked Cynthia to consider where she really wished she were in her life. What had her earlier dreams been? Where had she gone off course? What might she do if she could regain her health?

Cynthia had spent much of her life in denial. She had spent a great deal of energy denying her emotional pain, and this had led to her health seriously deteriorating. Her journey toward physical health would require a journey of emotional health.

Cynthia had not spent time reflecting. She had no one to be a cheerleader for her or coax another life from her. The cost to Cynthia is great—her body knows she is unhappy. Though she copes, she doesn't thrive. Denial—telling herself things aren't that bad—keeps her in a narrow, uncreative life. Breaking free means feeling her disappointment and loss, embracing her feelings, listening to God and herself about what might be waiting for her.

Denial for Cynthia, and perhaps you, both saves and kills. Denial—telling ourselves that our life is fine just the way it is—allows us to cope, adapt, and accommodate whatever comes our way. We watch as life passes us by, failing to fully engage in life or create the life we really desire.

Collusion

Most of us receive a lot of support for the life we live; few people are brave enough to question our decisions.

Friends and family watched Cynthia live a false, inauthentic life. They lived inauthentic lives as well, so they could not have cheered her on. They watched Cynthia cope with life. It wasn't their life or their responsibility to change it. They had their own lives to tend to, after all.

"My friends and family are in the same boat I'm in," she said. "Their lives aren't much better than mine, so they don't really push me forward. They give me clichés, like 'This is the way life is.' So I assume they're right."

"Do you really believe them?" I asked.

"I don't want to believe them," she said. "When I really listen to my disappointment and fear, I know I want more. If I listen to my body I know there is a healthier way of living."

"Yes," I said. "I wonder if you could find new friends to support you on your healing journey."

"I do have one person," she said excitedly. "I have a nutritionist who is helping me eat better as a way to help my thyroid and migraines. She counsels me too, and it seems to be helping."

"That sounds wonderful," I said. "I sense a spark of hope when you talk about that."

"Yes," she said slowly. "Judy, my nutritionist, says there are 'energy givers' and 'energy takers' in life and to be careful about who I associate with. I can find people clinging to their old lives just as I have, or I can find people who are stretching to discover their buried lives. That's what I want to do."

Julia Cameron, author of *Walking in this World* and her landmark book, *The Artist's Way*, says there will always be cheerleaders for our personal growth as well as those who are "wet blankets." The wet blankets collude with us as we stop growing, while the cheerleaders challenge us to move forward with our lives. She calls the naysayers "creative saboteurs," seeking to snobbishly derail us from our endeavors.

> Surviving a creative saboteur is like surviving a snakebite. It can be done and it makes a good story afterward. However, the first step—as with any snakebite—is to name and contain the poison. We cannot afford our own or anyone else's denial. We have been bitten. We have been poisoned.[5]

Naming Lost Parts

Before Cynthia could move forward with her life she had to take an inventory of where she had been and what she had lost. Much like a medical exam yielding a clear description of her pain and the problem along with the treatment plan, she had to review her life. I helped her do that.

Naming our lost parts is not an easy or clear journey. When we veer off course, the road we're on may seem to be right. Deep inside we may know we're not really living the life we were designed to live, but it has become our life. We have made it normal, and for a time, normal is okay.

I encouraged Cynthia to spend time quietly reflecting on who she was. I asked her to write out her life story, paying close attention to traumatic experiences, knowing these might hold clues that could be useful to her. These places of trauma could also contain buried emotion, issues needing to be experienced and grieved. Owning these could help in the healing process.

I asked her to pay close attention not only to the person she had become, but to the person she had *not* become. Had she longed to have a safe and loving home, filled with the laughter of children? Had she desired to take art lessons? Did she long to travel the world but never had the money to do so? What were the parts of her that were lost? This would be a painful journey, but it would be filled with opportunities and new insights.

I also asked her to embrace and seek to understand her physical symptoms. These were an integral part of her. It would be important not to attempt to push these away or deny them. Cynthia's symptoms were doing what they are intended to do—warn us that something is wrong. Her body aches cried out for attention, and she had a hunch these might not simply be medical problems, but symptoms of a life not being lived well.

Cynthia made several powerful and deeply positive decisions. She decided not to date and to dedicate her life to getting healthy. She sought and found a nutritionist to help her with that aspect of her life. She was also under her doctor's care, but wondered if she needed something more. She was certainly heading in the right direction.

From a Physician: Dr. Tyson Hawkins, Internist

Coping strategies. We use this term a lot in medicine. We talk to our patients about them. We refer patients to counselors to help patients develop them. We applaud patients who have them and decry those who don't. We often prescribe medication to those who feel they need "something to help them cope." We prefer the healthier variety of coping strategies such as exercise, meditation, and breathing, but unfortunately many of our patients have already developed unhealthy coping strategies that play a large role in their physical well-being. These include overeating, smoking, and substance abuse, to name a few.

These patients have learned to cope. But as my father shows

above, they have developed strategies to numb themselves and bury their feelings and are not truly experiencing life. They are uncomfortable with the anxiety and depression they experience and are looking for a way to make those less severe or go away altogether. They are afraid of these feelings, as they have been accompanied by significant pain in the past. We prescribe antidepressants, anxiolytics (tranquilizers), and sleeping aids so these people do not have to be alone with their thoughts. And often we succeed, for a time.

However, these medications, just like other coping strategies, can ultimately fail. As in Cynthia's example above, the body will often find ways to manifest these unresolved (and unattended) emotions. This typically leads to escalating doses of medications—carrying with them increased risks of side effects and dependence. Unless addressed head-on, these issues will bubble to the surface and command attention. In *The Body Keeps the Score*, Dr. van der Kolk says it this way, "Somatic symptoms for which no clear physical basis can be found are ubiquitous in traumatized children and adults." And, "Instead of feeling angry or sad, they experience muscle pain, bowel irregularities, or other symptoms for which no cause can be found." He also goes on to say, "Most seem to have made an unconscious decision that it is better to keep visiting doctors and treating ailments that don't heal than to do the painful work of facing the demons of the past."[6]

Lydia is a happily married elementary teacher who presented with fatigue, nausea, and early morning awakening. She would wake up early in the morning on most days with significant nausea, vomiting, and dry heaving. She could not keep down much food or drink. She was becoming exhausted and quite scared. She was convinced something was terribly wrong with her. She denied any significant history of anxiety and denied any particular problems in her job or home life. She was looking for answers.

We started a comprehensive medical evaluation with lab work and imaging. We discussed the possibility that her symptoms might be anxiety related, but she was quite adamant that was not the case. She did not "feel" anxious.

We saw each other frequently for a period of time while we ordered a series of tests. Workup was largely unrevealing and my suspicion for somatization grew. Each time we met, I would ask questions about her stress, work, and home life. I asked about her childhood and about any history of abuse. She continued to deny any overt history of trauma, but the more we talked, the more likely it became that she was struggling with unresolved anxiety. She had grown up in a Christian home and was always quite driven to succeed. She believed she had a supportive husband but admitted that she would have liked him to take her symptoms more seriously.

After several months of poorly controlled symptoms, she was ultimately willing to establish care with a counselor. I prescribed a low dose anxiolytic which proved to be quite beneficial and essentially resolved her symptoms. Over time she came to believe that her symptoms were psychosomatic in nature and related to her underlying anxiety. She has found significant benefit from counseling and medication and is no longer convinced there is something "terribly wrong with her."

Lydia's case is not atypical and is just one example of how underlying stress and anxiety, regardless of the root cause, can (and often does) manifest with myriad physical symptoms. Lydia is now working with her counselor to develop healthy coping strategies and healthy boundaries in her home life and at work. There is no doubt that medication can have a benefit in many of these situations, but I firmly believe it is not the whole answer and should be used only as an adjunct to true healing.

Recovering Your Lost Parts

You might think recovering your lost parts would be a relatively easy process; it is anything but that. Recovering lost parts is actually a process most do not undertake. Why? Because lost parts are just that—lost.

Remember Cynthia had lived a life filled with pain and trauma. She had experienced relationship stress from as early as she could remember. She had suffered from her parents' divorce, her father's numerous marriages, and her own two broken marriages.

She denied her grief, lowered her head, and plowed forward. In the process she had lost many opportunities other children are afforded. She had lost innocence, protection, and the safety needed to grow emotionally. She hadn't learned relationship skills that could serve her in her marriages. She had lost the opportunity to dream.

To recover her lost parts she had to go through a rather arduous process, as you must also do, involving the following steps:

1. Reflect on your life. Not everyone wants to take the time and energy to reflect on their life. Most have busy lives and can find a thousand reasons for not spending time quietly journaling and pondering who they are, where they have been, and where they want to go. You must spend considerable time reflecting if you are to gain any kind of perspective on your life.

2. As you reflect, consider how you were earlier in life and compare that to how you are now. This step involves reaching back and looking at the person you used to be. What were you like years ago? How have you changed? What have others said to you about changes they see in you? Make a note of what comes to you.

3. Grieve what you have lost. Yes, you must create space to consider and grieve what has been lost. You cannot make up lost time. You cannot regain youth. You can, however, grieve what you've lost so you clear space for moving forward.

4. Allow yourself to dream about who you would like to be in the future. After taking a glimpse of who you were and what you've lost, reflect on who you want to be. What might your best love life look like? What kind of work do you want to do? Where do you want to live, and how do you want to spend your time? Consider someone's life you admire and note what makes that life different from yours.

5. Embark on a journey to "live into" this new person. Now, put some feet to your dreams. Lay out the path you want to take and begin this new adventure. In this way you can recover what you have lost.

Everyone has lost parts. Everyone has regrets and wishes they could do some things over again. Those who thrive accept these regrets and live into the future. They recognize what has been lost, grieve it, and use these emotions to motivate them into positive change.

Coming Out of the Shadows

Cynthia struggled to recover her lost life, as most women do who have experienced relationship stress. Ongoing stress, as we have indicated, can be incredibly debilitating. Many of the memories of her losses are embedded deep within her psyche—such is the case for all of us.

Still, Cynthia embraced her challenge. Two broken marriages were enough to motivate her to recover her lost self. This involved parts of her that were lost and parts of her hidden in the shadows of her life, not clearly formed but seeking expression.

"Like I said, I'm not going to date. Actually, I'm going to date me. I'm going to be curious about who I am and who I want to be. I'm going to be so kind to myself and treat myself just the way I'd like a man to treat me. Does that sound strange?"

"It sounds delightful," I said. "Others will never treat us better than we treat ourselves. So love yourself well."

Cynthia worked with me for several months. We pored over her history and we both celebrated her life. She began going back to church, joined the choir, and began taking piano lessons. Her therapy became a safe container for all her pain. She is coming out of the shadows and into the light, and she is becoming the person she wants to be.

The Path Forward

Relationship stress is a robber. It steals your joy, your vibrancy, and in many cases your physical health.

Relationship stress is a secret, silent thief. Many don't know they have been victimized or, if they do know, they do not detect the full impact it has had on them. Stress takes parts of us that we must deliberately seek to recover. Recovery involves taking a reflective journey. If we take this deliberate, necessary journey, healing is possible.

Are you ready to take this journey? Let's begin with the next chapter where we will explore in depth the sense of Self and Self-denial along with the power of magical thinking, a unique form of denial and detachment.

FOUR

THE STRUGGLE FOR A SELF

There are three things extremely hard: steel,
a diamond, and to know one's self.

—BENJAMIN FRANKLIN

A number of years ago Christie and I built our dream home, only to discover it was not a dream and certainly didn't feel like a home. Complications in building, the size of the home, and the location turned out to be disquieting for us. So we went on a search to find home once again.

What began as a challenging task soon turned into an adventure, something both Christie and I like to do. We enjoy house hunting, and this was no exception.

After finding several homes that suited our tastes but not our pocket-books, our Realtors, Mike and Robin, took us down a twisting and turning "Alice in Wonderland" lane to the water's edge.

"It's small," Mike said, smiling. "But the view of Seattle is to die for, and David, you can practically launch your kayak from your front door. Can you handle that?"

Mike and Robin unlocked the door and stepped aside, allowing us to enter and take in our first glimpse of this 1920s cottage. While our former home was large and pretentious, this cottage screamed, "Come live in me!"

Simple and charming, the home seemed just the right size. This was the penultimate cottage on the lane, complete with sitting area facing the water, stone fireplace, and cozy bedroom upstairs.

"Yes, we know it's small," Robin said. "But it's just the two of you now. This cottage wraps itself around you like a warm blanket. What do you think?"

We could not hide our enthusiasm. It was wonderful. This cottage said, "I will hold you. I will take care of you. You can feel safe here."

Almost everything felt wonderful. Almost.

"Where can I do my writing?" I asked Christie anxiously when we were alone. "And what about my piano?"

"You can write there in front of the window overlooking the water," she said, pointing to the sitting area. "Your piano will fit nicely against that wall."

We bought that cottage, even though I wasn't convinced. Then we went through growing pains—first adding a study onto the end of the house where I could do my work, and then changing the upstairs inglenook into a full master suite. We dreamed our cottage into a new, lovely home that fully met our needs. We needed a place that would fully hold ourselves—and it would.

Like Goldilocks, we had been in a house far too big and then moved into a cottage too small. Through awareness and compromise, we created something "just right."

Christie and I are blessed to live where we live. We are delighted with our small home, nestled amid towering pine, fir, and cedar trees. With a small patch of beachfront, I'm able to kayak out to drop my crab pots or sail my small dinghy while Christie walks along the beach collecting beach glass. We can be ourselves, at peace and at home.

A Home for a Self

My story is about finding our true selves, which is rarely an easy task. It is about finding a place for your Self to be well, sometimes an even more difficult journey. It's about knowing what you feel, think, and want so you can go about getting it—aspects of our Self many lose when in a troubled relationship.

Not only must you have a home for your Self, but you must rediscover a Self that feels like home. Not only must you find a place you can settle into and decorate as you wish, but you must also go about the work of being at home within yourself. You must go about the work of healing from the harm that has occurred from troubled or troubling relationships. Finding a place outside yourself and within your Self to be at peace is what this chapter is about.

Our cottage became that place for Christie and me—a place for us to regain our peace. The large, modern house we thought would be perfect was anything but. What we had designed and built turned out not to be a haven for us. Though not right for us, it was a perfect place for the next owners. As in the Goldilocks story, our cottage is now just right—not too big and not too small.

In a manner of speaking, a house is a perfect metaphor for your Self. With many rooms, your Self has many different parts with different needs at different times, and you must become familiar with them. To fully know your Self you must create an emotional space filled with peace and safety. This sacred space holds your Self.

So far this book has emphasized that relationship stress can make you sick. This same stress can damage not only your physical well-being, but your Self, your core personhood. It is important that you learn to know and discover your Self, to recognize how you have been harmed.

You cannot heal what you do not understand. You cannot heal what you cannot feel. You cannot know what you need unless you spend considerable time and energy exploring exactly who you are and cultivating an awareness of the stress you are experiencing.

Loss of Self

There is perhaps nothing more debilitating than to lose a sense of Self—literally to lose your Self. To lose stability, clarity, and focus is to feel like you are losing complete control of your life. Add to that confusion a loss of physical stability, and you have a recipe for disaster.

In some ways your experience may not be too dissimilar from that of Helen Keller, the girl who, at the age of 19 months, contracted a viral infection that robbed her of her sight, hearing, and ability to speak. Can you imagine? Without words, sound, or sight, she had no ability to make sense of her world, rendering her unable to cultivate a sense of Self—perhaps similar to your experience.

Helen Keller would have been completely without hope were it not for a woman, Anne Sullivan, who took a keen interest in her. Sullivan tutored Helen, introducing her to the world of words and, most important, to other children who were blind and mute at the Perkins School for the Blind in Boston. Helen's discovery of words allowed her to share her deepest pain with another human being—a profound and moving experience.

This bridge of pain dramatically changed Helen's world. Sullivan painstakingly helped Helen put words to her pain, just as you must of yours.

During a recent marriage intensive, Janine, a 50-year-old client, reminded me of Keller's story. She and her husband, Daniel, had come to the Marriage Recovery Center to work intensively with me for three days. During their work, Janine repeatedly apologized for her lack of focus and ability to articulate what she was experiencing. Fumbling for words and struggling to connect her thoughts, she became more anxious as she tried to express herself.

A former marketing expert, Janine had enjoyed a fast-paced career with financial and creative rewards. She had excelled in the world of words and ideas. Now she sat embarrassed and tearful.

Her husband, Daniel, reached out his hand for support, but she pulled away. She repeatedly apologized.

"I'm sorry, I really have to pace myself during this intensive," she said tearfully. "I get so distracted and confused," she added. "I just have such a hard time focusing, and I have to listen closely to my body or I'll overdo it. If that happens I'll be in bed the rest of the day."

I was surprised at how Janine felt she was unable to tolerate any stress. She dabbed the tears from her eyes, crying as she spoke.

"This is *so* frustrating," she said, pounding her fist on her chair. "I've worked 16-hour days and managed a team of a hundred people. Now I can't work more than three or four hours, and if I'm not careful, I can't work at all. I can't seem to find the words to say what I want to say."

"What's changed?" I asked curiously.

"The stress in my marriage has done this to me," she said, turning to Daniel. "Daniel is so critical of me but insists he isn't doing anything wrong. He says I'm making too much of our problems. I think my relationship with my parents started all this. My mother's a real crazymaker and my father was a narcissist. I didn't learn about boundaries. I didn't learn how to take care of myself. I wasn't raised to know anything about boundaries, and now I struggle to set boundaries with Daniel. I've lost myself to everybody else's needs. I doubt myself and don't know who I am."

She paused.

"The worst part is literally not being able to think straight. It's really frustrating."

Janine spoke in generalities, but she used language I've heard from many other women. She spoke of losing her Self and meeting everyone else's needs to her own detriment. She was distracted, confused, and unable to clearly share how her husband and parents try to talk her out of feeling what she is feeling. She fights to be heard and fully understood. After many years of feeling unheard and worthless, she is depleted, confused, and exhausted.

Once vibrant and able to work under huge amounts of stress, she strives to nurse her Self back to health. She searches for the words to convey what she is experiencing, the words that create a home for her Self.

Double-Minded

Nursing her Self back to health would not be as easy as it might sound. Couldn't she simply set healthy boundaries on her parents, husband, and anyone else who causes her confusion and harm?

No!

Her task is not nearly that simple, and I suspect you understand that. If you've had any close relationship that offers great benefits at great cost, you can identify with her complex problem. While friends and even professionals offer simplistic counsel—"Leave him!"—her dilemma is not so easily solved.

She's also been advised to ignore the demands of her parents, but again, this is not as easy as it sounds. Janine loves her husband and parents. Her world is not so simple. She has mixed feelings. Her feelings of exhaustion amplify that confusion.

Janine may have experienced what the apostle James speaks about when discussing double-mindedness.

> When you ask, you must believe and not doubt, because the one who doubts is like a wave of the sea, blown and tossed by the wind...Such a person is double-minded and unstable in all they do (James 1:6-8).

Another version amplifies this concept: "Their loyalty is divided between God and the world, and they are unstable in everything they do" (NLT).

While Janine's faith is certain, she has divided loyalty between herself and others. She is divided between Self and others, between her values and the needs and values of others—between what she wants and what others want for her. This division creates profound inner chaos.

If Janine had only her Self to tend to, her task would be much simpler. She might be clearer about what she felt and wanted, able to articulate her needs. But her parents also clamor for her attention, adding confusion to her inner experience. Her husband constantly peppers her with needs and desires, causing her to question herself.

Janine felt pulled in a thousand directions. How could she possibly sort out all the voices and please everyone? She couldn't, and the stress of it all was literally killing her.

Porous Boundaries

Boundaries are the metaphorical fences we build to surround the yard that contains our Self. Our emotional fences contain us, hold us, and protect us. These boundaries—statements to others of what we value and insist upon—create safety. These emotional fences allow us to breathe a sigh of relief, knowing we are safe and protected. By setting boundaries we give ourselves permission to make decisions that allow us to heal.

Boundaries are imperative to healing and holding our Self. Boundaries create internal safety as we learn to truly trust ourselves. We must feel capable of saying to others, "Please don't tell me what I think or what I should do. Please tell me only what you think and what you want. Then, together, we can decide how we will work things out."

This, of course, is not the way most of our lives proceed. Our boundaries, often porous and unsettled, are easily violated, and we often, without thinking, violate others' boundaries. Others may presume it's okay, even helpful to assert their wishes and demands. We probably do the same at times. The result of this causes confusion, chaos, and, in some instances, trauma.

Emotional health is based upon safety—strong, clear, firm boundaries and a clear sense of Self. We must trust and know we can create a peaceful place to think clearly, know our emotions (or *e-motions*, energy in motion), and allow those emotions to inform us about what is important to us. Armed with such vital information we can move into the world with new words, concepts, and ideas.

Depletion

How can a person like Janine have lived such a vibrant life, filled with energy and possibility, and then land in a place where she is hardly able to navigate day-to-day activities? Perhaps you have been in such a place of abject confusion. When you don't have mental clarity, you don't have much.

We all experience stress and face pressures like juggling children, career, and running a home, and yet not all of us succumb to exhaustion, confusion, and depletion. Why was Janine so depleted?

Dr. George Simon shares in his article "Healing the Fractured Self," "Trauma victims can have their sense of what's real and what's safe severely undermined...It can also lead to deep divisions within them, creating uncertainties about themselves, their ability to cope, and the nature of their relationship to the outside world."[1]

Did this explain what was happening to Janine? I believe so. As I reviewed Janine's history, I saw clearly that she had been raised to be an achiever. Her parents were both professionals and expected her to be a professional woman, to ignore her feelings and perform—and perform she did.

She not only went to college but excelled there, pushing herself beyond normal limits. Not content with a bachelor of arts degree, she pushed herself to obtain her MBA, majoring in marketing. She rose quickly in the business world because of her hardworking nature and brightness. She demanded much from those who worked for her and, moreover, from herself.

"It wasn't just one thing that created my problems," she shared. "I handled a lot of pressure until constant conflict with Daniel pushed me over the top. He reminds me of my mother! First it was my parents who demanded so much from me, and now my husband. My mother is unbelievably critical and never satisfied. I didn't even realize how much like her Daniel was, but he always expected more and more from me. I lost myself both in my marriage and my relationship with my parents. No matter how hard I tried, I couldn't please any of them. I think that's what's killed me."

Janine's a classic case of a woman who slowly lost herself. Specifically, she lost her Self—her own boundaries that might have protected her values, desires, and needs. She lost her sense of well-being, her confidence, and belief that she could successfully navigate her world.

Self-Discovery

Janine is lost and alone, trying valiantly to regain her emotional and physical footing. Relationship stress can make you physically sick, to be sure, but besides adversely impacting your health, it also detrimentally impacts your sense of Self. How does this occur?

Peter Levine, in his book *In an Unspoken Voice*, says this of people who have struggled with excessive, chronic stress: "Trapped between feeling too much (overwhelmed or flooded) or feeling too little (shut down and numb) and unable to trust their sensations, traumatized people can lose their way. They don't feel like themselves anymore; loss of sensation equals a loss of a sense of self."[2]

Stress, and subsequent poor health, is a great distractor and limit setter. When laboring under stress we do not focus on our Self. We become either overwhelmed with body sensations or massively shut down by them, becoming very reactive and detached and disconnected.

We want to be free of these feelings created by stress but unfortunately respond in a habitual manner.

When working with couples in conflict I've noticed an alarming pattern: Most keep doing the same things, fighting in the same ways, over and over again. They are entrenched in conflictual patterns that not only keep them stuck in a very difficult bind but cause their health to suffer; and all the while they are unaware of what they are doing to themselves. They bicker and try to solve problems in the same ineffective ways, which only multiplies the distress. They become stuck in patterns of fighting, fleeing from themselves and their mate, or freezing—detaching from their Self.

In such a state of agitation and stress they cannot think straight. They cannot solve or find creative ways around problems. Subsequently, they do not grow or thrive. They cling to the life they have, which in far too many instances is no life at all.

Stress is the result of not functioning from your "best Self." That is, under stress, most slip habitually into *fight, flight,* or *freeze*—all incredibly detrimental to problem solving and growth.

Think about it. When I am faced with a threat, my brain goes into fight mode. The person or situation threatening me becomes the enemy. If you are the enemy, I am tempted to try to conquer you. The battle is on.

Perhaps your method of responding to stress is to freeze or flee. You withdraw from conflict. You run and hide, pull the covers over your head, hoping the problem will magically disappear. It doesn't, of course; and when you come out from hiding, the problem is still there, maybe even bigger than ever.

Can you see what is happening? Instead of being fluid in the moment, considering all options, and using your strong, creative Self, you have shrunk into helplessness. This can and must be changed.

David Gommé, in his article "The Only Way to Effectively Contain Stress," shares that we tend to overuse one or two coping strategies for stress when in fact we need an array of responses. He writes, "The most effective way to learn to use oneself properly—the shortest

short-cut, if you like—is in escaping the 'one thing' syndrome by edu-
cating oneself to exercise choice in response rather than auto-reacting
from one's habitual fight-flight instincts...The over-exertion upon a
small segment of the spectrum of our vast human potential causes the
equivalent of metal fatigue—mentally and emotionally so."

He advises the following approach: Take a step back from the stressful situation and take stock of how you react to stressful situations. To
what degree are you able to effectively respond to the demands of the
situation rather than being squeezed into a habitual response? What
does this particular situation need from you? What qualities do you
need if you are to handle the situation most effectively?[3]

Charles

We all want to be well. As the saying goes, "You can have everything,
but if you don't have your health, you have nothing."

This is true.

I am working with a man, Charles, who has more money than he
can ever spend. He has the finest clothes, the most incredible home,
the newest luxury car, and a concierge physician ready to help him with
his myriad health issues. Still, because he doesn't have his health, he
spends most days sitting home essentially waiting to die.

Charles is not suicidal, but he has lost his health and his will to
really live. He is significantly overweight, suffers from high blood pressure, and uses food to ease his pain. Lost in his small world of food, he
is unhappy, lethargic, and discouraged.

Living in an embittered marriage has left him cranky. He says
he and his wife live separate lives, having argued for years, and now
choose to simply live as "roommates." Did his wife make him cranky,
or has he made his wife unhappy? The interplay between his health,
marriage, and mental health is clear—he is not dealing with problems effectively and is coping in some very primitive ways. He is not
a happy man.

Charles is also distant from his three grown children. This is no
surprise, since he has invested little time in their lives or his grand-
children's lives. While he is a father and grandfather, he has done little

active fathering. Charles has retreated as a way to cope with his emotional pain.

Charles is close to no one. He came to counseling knowing he needed to change. He lives superficially, attached to no one. Upon meeting him you'd feel his sarcastic, biting edge. You'd know he was depressed and anxious just below the surface, and you would likely tiptoe around him. He offers no invitation to come close.

As Bessel van der Kolk says in *The Body Keeps the Score*, "People who feel safe and meaningfully connected with others have little reason to squander their lives doing drugs or staring numbly at television; they don't feel compelled to stuff themselves with carbohydrates or assault their fellow human beings."[4] Charles is squandering his life. He is unhappy, and his physical problems only add to his emotional and relational ones. In addition to being unhappy, Charles is tired, like so many women coming to me with relationship stress. He is anxious from the inner battle waging in his mind every day. He is weary and lethargic from the layers of protection that have served to isolate him from himself and the outside world.

Illness as Protection

While most of my clients suffering from stress and emotional abuse and in their relationships are women, there are men, too, who suffer from stress and emotional abuse.

Charles is passive, lonely, and isolated. He is doing little to change his life or actively work on his weight or blood pressure. Caught in an endless pattern of tiredness, excessive weight, and stress eating, he listens only superficially to the counsel of his physician. "Of course I know I need to exercise and eat differently to lose weight," he shared with me, "but I am not motivated to do it. It's a vicious circle—the more weight I gain, the worse I feel, and the worse I feel, the more weight I gain."

Charles shrugged in disgust.

"Everyone has 'the answer' for me too," he said. "Everyone thinks it should be so easy to lose weight."

"It's pathetic, I know," he continued. "I'm smarter than I'm acting, that's for sure. I used to be a 'can-do' guy and now I'm a 'can't-do' guy. It's very frustrating."

Could it be that Charles' weight is a symptom or perhaps even protection against deeper emotional pain? Does he eat to soothe his pain or perhaps add weight to insulate himself from the world?

Charles is unhappy and unhealthy—in marriage and in life. He describes his wife as critical and demanding. His response is either to snap back at her or withdraw from her. Like many women I work with, Charles is either passive or aggressive, struggling to speak his mind. Over many years he has lost his voice. His sense of Self is very uncertain or even nonexistent.

In an odd way, Charles' weight and blood pressure issues have become an identity for him. His thoughts revolve around food and his illness. He obsesses about these problems yet does nothing to change them.

Sadly, Charles' weight and blood pressure may serve to protect him, offering him a weak sense of Self and reason for being. He withdraws from his wife rather than dealing directly with his feelings about her incessant criticism. He previously poured himself into his work, though since retiring he now uses food and the television to escape. This has, sadly, become his new identity.

Like Janine, Charles lost his Self. He lost it by overeating, becoming "numb," and withdrawing from life rather than facing his problems. As with Janine, relationship stress is killing him, and he feels trapped in a vicious cycle: He is too tired and discouraged to invest time in things like counseling, exercise, and healthy nutrition changes that would alleviate his pain.

From a Physician: Dr. Tyson Hawkins, Internist

"Tell me about yourself."

This is a pretty common opening line when I first meet a patient. It is meant to be vague and open-ended, leaving room for the patient to talk about what they do for work, their family, their upbringing, their hobbies, or their medical history. While we as physicians care about the patient as a person, we also understand that you are there for a reason. We understand it is not a social call. We're ultimately looking for a list of medical diagnoses and current ailments that will help frame the patient and guide the direction of our visit. We are unintentionally asking patients to identify themselves by their past and current health conditions.

It is always interesting to hear how patients answer this question. Some patients lead by saying, "I know I'm fat and that a lot of my medical problems would probably get better if I lost some weight." Others might simply say, "I work for the transit authority and have three kids." The way they answer this simple question says a lot about them and how they identify (or don't identify) themselves with their disease.

Let's take the obese patient as an example. When I probe deeper into their struggles with weight, I am not surprised to hear about their personal challenges with stress. Often it can be a history of abuse, whether emotional, physical, or sexual. It can be their marriage. It can be their kids. It can be their parents, or their job. One thing is certain, though—there is *always* a stressor. They will go on to talk about how they eat because it makes them feel better, or that they do not have enough energy to exercise. Or that exercise hurts. When somebody lives with a condition long enough, I believe they start to identify themselves with the condition. They are one and the same. It becomes harder and harder to separate the person from the condition.

I met Bill five years ago. He was transferring care to me after his previous primary care provider retired. He was morbidly obese with a body mass index greater than 50, with multiple coconcurring conditions, including poorly controlled type II diabetes, hypertension, sleep apnea, and chronic lymphocytic leukemia (CLL). He was gruff, to say the least, and had burned bridges with previous care providers and staff due to his attitude. At one point he was asked to fill out a behavioral contract.

Bill identifies himself by his obesity and as a victim of other people's prejudice. He blames the way he feels on his obesity but is angry when others do so. Instead of searching for the underlying cause of his overeating and food addiction, he spends his energy on anger and indignation. He is always looking to pick a fight. I don't know for sure what started Bill on this downward spiral of unhealthy habits, but I do know that his attitude plays a big role in keeping him there.

Bill's low point came several years ago when his wife passed away; and he has been a different man since. He has been more vulnerable and willing to discuss his feelings more openly. He admits that his weight and his many medical problems scare him. He is now much more willing to ask for help.

I believe Bill has been defined by his illness—obesity. He is fed up with everybody telling him he needs to lose weight and blaming how he feels on his physique. He has spent many years making others feel guilty for judging him. I believe he has been afraid to look at the deeper issues, insecurities, and fears, and instead has found it safer to focus on how others have treated him. This attitude only served to worsen the quality of his medical care, not improve it.

When asking my patients about their deeper pain, anxieties, or current stressors, I sometimes hear patients tell me that dealing with their stress and anxiety is just too hard. They are seeking an easier way, and often that leads to unhealthy habits. Overeating is a common one, and an easy one to identify; it's hard to hide your weight. But people manage their stress and anxieties in many ways that are less overt. They might admit when confronted, however, that they are too afraid to pursue the root cause of their symptoms. They recognize their coping mechanisms are unhealthy, but they are afraid to dig deeper. Identifying themselves by their illness has allowed them to ignore their deeper hurt and pain.

Healing Through Boundaries

Charles and Janine both lack healthy boundaries, which only adds to their problems. Boundaries offer definition to our lives, a home for our Self. We define ourselves by our authenticity—what we prefer and what we don't prefer. When we feel healthy, we think clearly, articulate our needs, and feel a sense of personal agency—an ability to influence our world.

This world of setting, maintaining, and managing personal boundaries is, however, an arduous task. It takes focus that, when we are feeling stressed, is usually in short supply.

What must Janine and Charles do?

They must have the inner fortitude—guts—to grab a dose of conviction and decide to speak out. They must find the ability to say yes and no to various issues in their lives.

Janine must learn to say no to the demands of her parents and husband. She must determine what is important to her and what will bring joy back to her life. She must feel conviction and act on that conviction, insisting on a safe space to be who she is called to be. Then, and only then, will some of her stress subside so she can experience a new life, a new Self.

Likewise, Charles must stop retreating from his troubled marriage and seeking relief in carbohydrates and mindless television. He must break through his denial of marriage problems and an eating disorder and understand he is destroying his life. Losing weight and gaining confidence in himself, he can find strength to face issues in his marriage. Slowly he will begin to feel healthier, and health begets health. Changing habits reaps benefits.

Self-Talk

This journey toward physical and emotional well-being is ultimately a battle of the mind. I teach that "Self" is a composite of our boundaries and the relationships we allow to exist within those boundaries. Now let's add another component—our relationship with ourselves.

Scripture states that as a man (or woman) thinks, so they are (Proverbs 23:7). In other words, our thoughts lead to our feelings, which often culminate in actions. These actions then lead back to feelings and thoughts. Confusing? It certainly can be.

The key point here is that we are healthier, or less healthy, depending on how we view and think about the world. If we are clear and function from a place of integrity and conviction, we will likely be healthy. If, however, we have misbeliefs about ourselves and the world, we are likely to become unhealthy.

Scripture is certainly right when it implores, "You will know the truth, and the truth will set you free" (John 8:32). The key is to discover the truth and then allow it to set us free—something many of us do not do.

William Backus and Marie Chapian, in their book *Telling Yourself the Truth,* state, "Misbeliefs are the direct cause of emotional turmoil, maladaptive behavior and most so-called 'mental illness.' Misbeliefs are the cause of the destructive behavior people persist in engaging in even when they are fully aware that it is harmful to them (such as overeating, smoking, lying, drunkenness, stealing or adultery). Misbeliefs generally appear as truth to the person repeating them to himself...This is partly because they often do contain some shred of truth."[5]

Persistent painful feelings are not part of a healthy sense of Self or a healthy relationship.

Reflecting again upon Janine and Charles's life, what are some of their Self-destructive misbeliefs?

- "I am making too much of these problems."
- "I shouldn't be feeling such confusion."
- "They are right and I am wrong."
- "There is something wrong with me."
- "My feelings cannot be trusted."

Can you see how each of these misbeliefs led them into feeling even more anxiety and confusion? What can they say to lead themselves back to sure footing?

- "My feelings are natural and healthy."
- "Anyone would feel confused if they struggled with my husband/wife and family."
- "I'm right to be feeling what I'm feeling."

- "My feelings can be trusted and can lead me."

Janine and Charles have their work cut out for them. They must sort out what others say to them and what they determine to be their truth. They must struggle to find their Self and to discover what they truly believe, as opposed to what others believe. Recognizing their voice as distinct from the voice of others is an excellent place to begin.

Too Many in My Head

Getting healthy means getting clear about who we are and what we think. Getting healthy is about becoming a solid individual, separate from others. This is Janine's and Charles's task.

In Alcoholics Anonymous we hear about "the committee," or different thoughts and feelings swirling around in our heads, often giving us conflicting messages or bad advice. Members of "the committee" must be identified and called out, named for who they are, and deliberately fired.

Becoming emotionally sober and physically healthy means becoming keenly acquainted with those voices. We often have so many people giving us advice that we don't know what we think.

Most of us are surrounded by people all too willing to tell us what to do, think, and feel. These people may presently be in our lives, or our minds may be cluttered with voices from our past—parents, siblings, mates, friends.

Who are some of the people in your "committee" of voices? Here are a few for you to be on the watch for and to subsequently eliminate from your head.

The Critic. This voice tells you that you are doing things wrong. There is a right way to do things and the way you're doing them is not it. The Critic may be subtle, as in "Why did you do that?" or blatant, as in "You're making a big mistake by doing that." Their advice is unsolicited and therefore always feels like criticism, which it is.

The Shamer. This voice uses words such as *should, ought,* and *must,* catching us when we do anything that violates this code of conduct. Unfortunately, these rules for living often come from someplace other than our authentic Self. This voice comes from parental messages, authority figures, mates, and friends. These guilt-inducing voices need to be silenced and updated with our true feelings and beliefs.

The Denier. This voice tries to convince us that everything we're doing is working for us, when this is definitely not the case. This voice tells us not to worry, that everything will magically work out. Problems are minimized or denied, or, worse, blamed on others. We escape responsibility, but in the process we also escape the possibility for positive change.

The Ego. This voice wants what it wants when it wants it, and believes it is entitled to have it. Others are overpowered in the process, and even our best Self is silenced by this powerful, self-centered voice. The Ego is immature, selfish, and will think and act in childish ways that are certain to hurt your better Self.

The Generalized Other. This voice is actually another committee—"all those people out there." We fear what "everyone" will think. We worry about how others will view us. We are often paralyzed by the beliefs we project onto the world and what the world might believe about us.

Can you see how damaging the committee is to our individuality and healing our Self? Can you see that the committee must be identified, listened to, and then silenced in favor of our true and strong Self?

Brain Fog, Fatigue, and Recovery

Listening to the committee is not just tiring; it is harmful to our brain. The ultimate impact of being taunted by the committee is what we call *brain fog*—an inability to think straight or make healthy decisions in one's best interest. Too many voices, given too much power and influence, have the power to render us confused and very anxious.

Remember, we must cultivate our ability to have our own thoughts, judgment, and reasoning if we are to navigate this world. Others can never tell you what is best for you. Others can never tell you what you value, what you think, or the decisions you must make. You alone know what is right, true, and good for you, and you must ultimately make those decisions for yourself.

Other voices, if given too much authority, create noise, and that results in brain fog and fatigue. This noise, combined with emotional and physical stress, leads to even greater degrees of anxiety and often panic.

While brain fog may sound benign, it is anything but. We must be able to rely on our reasoning abilities. Brain fog is the destroyer of our Self and ultimately our reasoning abilities. Brain fog is the result of intense anxiety, over a long period of time, combined with issues of dis-ease.

Fortunately, pushing away from the committee and turning down the volume on internal and external noise helps regain a sense of Self. Listening carefully to what *you* think, what *you* want, and what *you* believe to be right and true for your Self can restore you to healthy functioning.

The Path Forward

While you may have heard or believed that attending to your Self is selfish, it is anything but. I challenge you to embrace a new definition of Self. Your healing path must contain selfishness—intensive self-care—as you strive to regain your emotional and physical balance.

Rather than being selfish, time and attention paid to your Self will pay rich dividends in the form of self-awareness and self-love, which lead to understanding your true thoughts and feelings. Armed with information, you are able to make stronger, wiser choices.

Healthy self-love and care for your Self enable you to give generously to others. When you are well, you see others through a kind and loving lens.

Let's continue our journey toward understanding the true impact of relationship stress on your mind and body.

Five

What You've Never Been Told About Stress

PTSD is a whole-body tragedy, an integral
human event of enormous proportions
with massive repercussions.

—SUSAN PEASE BANITT

What if much of what you've learned about stress is wrong?

As much as we complain about stress, most of us know very little about it. Sure, we've all complained about being "stressed out." We've told ourselves we must lower our stress.

When our friends tell us they're stressed out, we nod in quick agreement, just as they do when we complain about the stress in our lives. We offer words of encouragement and receive those same words in return.

But what if stress, and managing it, is far more complex than we've been taught?

This chapter will offer insight into a kind of stress we seldom hear about, but before we begin looking at that, let's do a quick review.

We've all been taught that stress is a normal part of life. Check. We've been taught we must get plenty of sleep, eat a healthy diet, and exercise regularly. Check. We've been taught we must take control of our lives. Check. If overwhelmed, we've been taught to breathe deeply, try progressive muscle relaxation, and practice time management. Check.

These are the basics of stress management. And these points are good information. We must take control of our lives or our lives will take control of us. But what do we do when the stress in our lives requires more than the basics?

What You Already Know About Stress

You probably already know stress is debilitating. You know you must take control of your life. Though easier said than done, you undoubtedly attempt to do just that.

You know stress is cumulative, that stress, over time, can adversely impact your emotional life and even your physical health. There is much you already know, perhaps including these points:

- Much of the population experiences significant stress on a regular basis.

- Stress is a major cause of insomnia, chest pains, cardiac issues, depression, anxiety, and other psychosomatic problems.

- Stress triggers the body to send adrenaline and cortisol into the bloodstream, readying us for a fight-or-flight response.

- Reaction to stress makes the blood thicker and more viscous, which can lead to a blood clot. This response is intended to prepare us for urgency but can actually kill the healthy brain.

- Stress makes us physiologically ready for an emergency and so, for the short term, it is helpful.

Yes, you already know quite a bit about common stress, including its horrific impact on the mind and body. Now, let's add to your knowledge and open the door to learning what you don't know.

Myths About Stress

Before we get to our new definition of stress, I'd like to share a few myths.

1. *People respond to stress the same.* Wrong. We make a huge mistake by talking about stress as if it is the same for

everyone. It isn't. What is stressful for one person may not be stressful for another.

2. *All stress is the same.* Very wrong. Stress for many means waiting in a traffic jam for two hours. For another, it's having more month than money. For many reading this book, stress means chronic, health-debilitating agony. It means never knowing when life is going to return to normal.

3. *Stress strategies work the same for everyone.* Again, wrong. While some popular stress-reducing techniques may work for some people, they won't work for everyone. Again, we are all different and respond to stress differently. Subsequently, stress-reducing strategies must be tailored to fit a person's situation.

4. *Symptoms of stress are obvious.* Wrong. Stress has been called "the silent killer" since it can lead to heart disease, high blood pressure, chest pain, and irregular heartbeat. Symptoms are often unseen, ignored, denied, or misunderstood.

5. *We have choices about our stress.* Right and wrong. While it is true that we all have choices about our lives and lifestyle, many of us are in very difficult situations without easy answers. Many of us are in untenable circumstances where we must choose between highly challenging options.

We must look at stress differently. My sons and I want you to view stress from a more critical perspective. Subsequently we will categorize stress into three sections—*stress, post-traumatic stress,* and *complex post-traumatic stress*, emphasizing the third.

Different Kinds of Stress

Stress is generally thought of as a state of emotional strain resulting from an adverse or very demanding circumstance—something we are not fully prepared to handle, like being unprepared for a deadline on a paper that is due, facing legal problems, or raising a challenging teenager. We face stressful situations all the time.

Now let's raise the bar.

Post-traumatic stress occurs when we are facing a terrifying event, either by experiencing it or witnessing it. Symptoms include flashbacks, nightmares, and severe anxiety. The term originated with veterans experiencing war situations, extreme circumstances that were outside their customary experiences.

Post-traumatic stress disorder (PTSD) is a mental health problem some develop after experiencing or witnessing a life-threatening event such as combat, a natural disaster, or sexual assault.

Finally, we come to *complex post-traumatic stress*, a much more debilitating kind of stress that results from chronic or long-term exposure to emotional trauma—a central topic of this book. Complex post-traumatic stress disorder (complex PTSD) occurs when a victim has little or no control over their stress and subsequently feels little or no hope for escape.

A Crazy Kind of Stress

This new kind of stress, complex PTSD, is a more severe form of stress that is not often talked about. How can we compare it to common stress?

Talking about complex PTSD and its association to stress is like comparing a new winter dusting of snow to a February blizzard in upstate New York. It's like comparing a light breeze to a category-five hurricane.

There is *no* comparison. There is no commonality and no linking of the terms together.

Complex PTSD is stress to the tenth power—a crazy kind of stress. It can hardly even be talked about in the same breath as "normal stress" because it is so debilitating.

Imagine being caught in a category 5 hurricane, emphasis on the word *caught*. Imagine being in the direct path of life-threatening winds and torrential rains. There is no route of escape. Your only path of escape, meager as it is, is mental.

You tell yourself, *I'll make it through this.*

You repeat, *I'll live through this, one way or another.*

Of course, you don't fully believe this. Repeating these words is simply a way of numbing yourself against the onslaught of terror. If you allowed yourself to feel everything you're capable of feeling, you fear you might go crazy. So you go numb—again and again.

It's likely that you're familiar with PTSD, typically resulting from short-lived trauma such as a car accident or natural disaster. Complex PTSD stems from chronic, long-term exposure to trauma in which the victim has little control, and which they believe will never end, such as child abuse or long-term domestic violence or emotional abuse.

Chronic relationship stress often includes emotional abuse and often involves complex PTSD. As one resource puts it, "For those who experience this in adulthood, being at the complete control of another human being (often unable to meet their most basic needs without them), coupled with there being no foreseeable end in sight, is what breaks down their psyche and affects them far more severely than the trauma alone."[1]

What are some of the symptoms of complex PTSD (C-PTSD)—this wildly crazy kind of stress?

- *Emotion Regulation.* Relationship stress is typically fraught with wild emotions. Those struggling with C-PTSD have a difficult time both experiencing emotions and managing them. They may experience chronic sadness or explosive anger, and they may even be suicidal at times. It is very common for those surviving C-PTSD to feel numb, having blocked out feelings for so long they now struggle to know and manage their feelings. At times they feel like they're going crazy.

- *Difficulty with Self-Perception.* In severe relationship stress, typically involving complex PTSD, people often experience intense conflict; and where there is intense conflict, there is likely to be blame-shifting by the abuser. Blame-shifting is not troubling simply because someone is not taking responsibility for their actions, but also because you, the innocent one, are being told you're doing something wrong. Self-doubt creeps in and is played upon by your mate who foists their perceptions on you. Subsequently, your self-perception is shaken.

- *Did I bring this upon myself?*
- *Is it me?*
- *What did I do to deserve this?*

These are common questions. This shaken and confusing self-perception leads to disorientation.

- *Interruptions in Consciousness.* This is a very frightening aspect of C-PTSD. Some reliving traumatic events become so frightened they dissociate. Dissociation occurs on a spectrum that can range from harmless daydreaming and memory gaps to feeling disconnected from one's body or mental processes. Episodes of missing time occur, in which individuals "lose" minutes or days in their lives. This loss of a cohesive sense of self leads to feelings of significant confusion and, ultimately, feelings of craziness.

- *Difficulty with Relationships.* Those challenged with C-PTSD often feel completely isolated from others and struggle to know how to engage in a meaningful way. With their history of being betrayed, they struggle to trust others. Some have the exact opposite problem—trusting anyone far too easily, including those who are dangerous. Critical of their own judgment, they wonder if they are emotionally unstable or insane.

- *Inaccurate Perception of One's Perpetrators.* While it may seem crystal clear to others, survivors of C-PTSD don't necessarily have a clear view of the one causing them so much distress. Imagine a love-hate relationship, where the sufferer wants to get away from the abusive partner while also longing for their affections and acceptance. These conflicting thoughts are not easy on them; they lead to much confusion and ultimately exhaustion. These "can't live with them, can't live without them" experiences may leave them feeling as if they're going crazy.

- *Broken System of Meanings* (a set of relationships between a group such as behaviors and the meanings attached to them). The individual who has experienced chronic emotional abuse often finds it impossible to believe life will ever be normal. They doubt justice will ever be served, or even that God will protect them. They lose faith and trust in humanity, doubting there is any goodness or kindness in the world. During their worst times they wonder if they have been brought into the world to be hurt.[2]

Julie

Julie's life has changed dramatically as the result of being diagnosed with C-PTSD. Her struggle was palpable, and it affected every area of her life.

Julie is 45 years old and has been married to Sam for 20 years. While their marriage has been "rocky" from the start, the past two years have been very difficult.

"I have been unhappy for years," Julie said, "but I figured our problems were just like other couples'. I didn't know how bad things were until my body started to react to the constant fighting in our marriage. My husband is constantly critical of me and our kids."

"What is happening in your marriage?" I asked.

"Sam!"

"What do you mean?" I asked.

"Sam," she repeated. "It's Sam. He creates chaos in everything he does. He is angry, demanding, and always on edge. I'm embarrassed to say that my moods match his. If he's happy, our family is happy. If he's upset for any reason, my nerves go crazy and I'm mad."

Julie paused and went on to share that she had tried to live a normal life.

"I just can't live a normal life," she continued. "Sam is like a cyclone, and I spin around when he spins. It's horrible. I keep hoping he'll grow up, but that's not going to happen."

Julie shared more of her story, complaining about having two identities: One a loving, kind, and caring mother of three teenagers; and another a sickly, angry, combative woman, reacting to her husband's moods.

"I can live a pretty normal life," she said. "If things are going well in my marriage, I can be active, relatively healthy, and productive."

"I hate it when my C-PTSD flares up," she said. "Sam just has poor judgment. Just a few weeks ago he complained about me to our friends. I ask for his support and understanding, and he purposely goes to our friends and complains about me—and they listen!"

"What does he do?" I asked, sensing Julie knew much about C-PTSD.

"He goes out with our church friends and complains about *my* anger," she said. "He doesn't talk about *his* anger or crazymaking. We had agreed we would only talk about this with our therapist. I'm perfectly willing to talk about my anger and take ownership for it. But when Sam goes to our friends, who all talk and are my friends, I go ballistic. Then all my symptoms flare up, and I'm on the couch for days."

"What kinds of symptoms do you have?" I asked.

"My fibromyalgia really fires up and I hurt all over for days. I get migraines and I'm stuck in bed. I can't think straight. I'm furious at Sam, thinking about getting even with him, of going to all our friends and talking about him. But that would be crazy and I'd just look bad."

She paused.

"He knows better than to do these kinds of things," she said. "We've talked about them over and over. We've talked about them in front of you. He agreed to protect me, but I simply can't trust him. I have no hope of him getting better, so how can I get better? When my symptoms flare I can't even take care of simple chores around the house. Our boys eat frozen dinners and I'm furious at Sam, who just doesn't get it."

"What does he say when you confront him?" I asked.

"He apologizes pathetically," she said. "He looks at me all innocent and says he didn't really say that much. But the more I ask, the more he reveals, and everything points to me as the bad guy. He's more than willing to paint himself in a bright light and me in a dark one. It's infuriating. He doesn't take responsibility for any of it, and I feel completely alone."

"Scapegoated," I said. "Sam does know these boundaries. We've gone over them many times. He knows not to talk to your friends about these issues."

"So," she continues, "I never feel completely safe with him, and my feeling of hopelessness makes my C-PTSD erupt. I'm never sure he gets it and can be trusted to protect me."

"Yes, Julie," I said. "Let's set up another session with you and Sam and go over this. He needs to develop better boundaries, protect you, and take ownership for his behavior. He needs to understand the impact his behavior has on you."

Loss of Hope

Damage had been done.

Can you see it? Can you understand why Julie doesn't feel completely safe and secure? She has set boundaries with Sam and he has repeatedly violated them, leaving her vulnerable to his poor judgment and harmful behavior. He protects himself at her expense.

She faces nearly impossible choices about whether to stay with Sam or start life over. The life she has known is intertwined with a man who is harmful to her well-being. She feels ambivalent about how to proceed.

C-PTSD is about experiencing an outer sense of chaos leading to an inner world of craziness. It's about having lost the sense that you are, more or less, in control of your world. Julie has lost her inner sense of stability and predictability.

All of us can manage temporary stress. As much as we hate it, we know the storm will pass. Even those in Florida, Louisiana, and Texas experiencing the horrors of hurricanes know the storms will pass and the people left behind will set about rebuilding. They know the external chaos will lead to *temporary* internal chaos, but they will marshal their resources, pull together, and rebuild their lives.

This never happens with C-PTSD, because part and parcel of this disorder is the chronicity of the stress. It is the belief they will never fully manage their stress because it is outside of their control. They cannot stop the pain.

It seems only yesterday I was having a conversation with my older son, Joshua, who was in the third year of his five-year surgical residency. He told me about the 100-hour workweeks, working while painfully ill, and yet having absolutely no recourse.

I rose to protective-father mode.

"Perhaps you need to consider an alternative course, son," I said.

He responded impatiently.

"Dad, I've chosen this career. Everyone goes through it. I have to lower my head and get it done. There is no way out, just through it."

"Maybe it's time to consider a different specialty," I said, thinking I was offering hope.

"Please, Dad. You are not understanding me. I'm in this and have to see it through."

He didn't need me to brainstorm solutions. There were none. He had only one choice: Finish his residency and get to the other side.

Even his stress, as phenomenal as it was, was not C-PTSD, because *there was an end to it.*

What if there is no end? What if any path appears to be a dead end? What then?

Outer Chaos, Inner Chaos

Let's talk more about Julie.

Her husband, Sam, gathers with his buddies for coffee and tells himself he is "just sharing with friends." He shares about his wife's anger and minimizes his part in their marital problems. He gives no thought to the fact he has agreed not to share details of their marriage to others without his wife's consent.

Having normalized his actions, he becomes defensive when Julie confronts him about what he has done. He scolds her for trying to control whom he can talk to, making her out to be a controlling woman (scapegoating). When confronted, he becomes instantly irritated, scapegoating and blaming her, creating even more internal and external chaos for Julie. He is in massive denial about his actions that cause her so much distress.

Sam declined a couple's session, but a week later Julie and I met again.

"How has it gone with Sam?" I asked.

"He doesn't see any of the damage he has done," she said. "He's mad at me for making a mountain out of a molehill—but it's no molehill. I'm really discouraged."

"He says he's just getting support from friends," she continued, "defending everything he has done. I feel hopeless."

"He couldn't see the harm he caused you by talking to your friends?"

"Nope," she said. "He promised me he wouldn't talk to our friends about our problems. I don't trust him not to put his spin on things."

Spin is right. Julie's head is spinning and her external world is spinning wildly too, leading to inner chaos.

"I told Sam that he didn't just talk to friends, he talked about me and our marriage. But that's not how he sees it. We agreed he would not talk about *my* anger with his friends. We agreed when he did, he paints himself as the innocent one and me as the lunatic. We agreed to work on these issues with someone we both can trust, Dr. Hawkins. *This is not what we agreed.*"

We invited Sam to the next session. Sam continued to defend himself, creating even more chaos.

"You're overreacting, Julie," he said. "I slipped up and I'm sorry. But you don't have to be so upset about it. It's not that big a deal."

Julie looked to me for help.

"She's right about this, Sam," I said. "You broke an agreement, painted her in a negative light, and now you need to own up, take responsibility, and fix things. She's now experiencing the fallout from your actions."

"What fallout?" he continued defensively.

"Fibromyalgia, migraines, loss of energy, and fighting with you!" she said. "I don't have the energy for all this. You have to protect me. You have to keep your promises."

Self-Confidence

Julie's life was out of control, leading to stress, PTSD, and ultimately complex PTSD. Her life had been relatively stable for the past few weeks, providing a respite from her fibromyalgia symptoms. Now, at the time of her meeting with me, she reported struggling to keep her emotional life balanced and finding it nearly impossible.

Julie was scrambling to pick up the emotional pieces. Sam didn't make it any easier for her. Sitting in my office, she was frozen by her problems. As if watching a line of dominoes fall, she could do little at the moment to fix things, leading to an increasing sense of hopelessness and loss of self-confidence.

We cannot say enough about the impact of the loss of hope. We are all bolstered by the belief that we can positively influence our personal world, leading to feelings of self-confidence. This is something many often take for granted; people like Julie relish their momentary feelings of empowerment. We must have the sense we can generally control our world. We must know we can solve the problems that come our way. Without this self-confidence, we become prone to depression, anxiety, and physical distress.

When I think about self-confidence I appreciate my sense of belief that I can generally accomplish whatever I hope to do. Evaluating my self-worth and abilities, I trust in my ability to achieve the goals I set before myself. This is *not* the world of those suffering from C-PTSD.

Quite the opposite.

Psychologists have long praised self-confidence as a trait that greatly decreases nervous tension, alleviates fear, and increases a sense of well-being. When self-confidence is lost, a host of negative symptoms floods in.

Unfortunately, all of this becomes a vicious cycle—chronic stress leads to lowered self-esteem and self-confidence. Dr. Neel Burton, in his article "Building Confidence and Self-Esteem," says, "In later life, self-esteem can be undermined by ill health, negative life events such as losing a job or getting divorced, deficient or frustrating relationships, and a general sense of lack of control."

Dr. Burton goes on to say, "People with low self-esteem tend to see the world as a hostile place and themselves as its victim. As a result, they are reluctant to express and assert themselves, miss out on experiences and opportunities, and feel powerless to change things. All this lowers their self-esteem still further, sucking them into a downward spiral."[3]

This certainly describes Julie's world. She is faced with a huge challenge—holding her husband accountable for the boundaries they've agreed upon. As she does so, and he keeps his agreements, she will feel safe and secure, and her self-confidence will grow.

From a Physician: Dr. Tyson Hawkins, Internist

Complex PTSD is also known as a dissociative subtype of PTSD. The diagnosis of dissociative PTSD can be made if, in addition to the full symptoms of PTSD, the individual has depersonalization (feeling detached from or as though one were an outside observer of one's own mental processes or body) and/or derealization (the world seeming unreal or dreamlike).[4] Patients with complex PTSD often have a history of PTSD earlier in life, more trauma exposure, and higher rates of suicide.

There are thought to be two subtypes of trauma in children and adults. Type 1 trauma results from predominantly single traumatic experiences, like a car accident, combat, and assault. Type 2 trauma is typically associated with prolonged exposure to extreme stressors (recurrent verbal, emotional, sexual, or physical abuse). Type 1 trauma is more likely to result in the development of hyperarousal subtype PTSD, where people respond to triggers with hypervigilance, increased cortisol release, flashbacks, palpitations, and sweating. Type 2 trauma is more likely to result in the development of complex PTSD, often associated with a decreased or blunted autonomic response, decreased heart rate, decreased cortisol release, and, as previously mentioned, symptoms of depersonalization or derealization.

PTSD is fairly common, occurring in 6.8 to 12.3 percent of the population, with complex PTSD accounting for 15 to 30 percent of those cases. While PTSD and complex PTSD are not uncommon, they are likely underdiagnosed and underappreciated. Complex PTSD is associated with a higher risk of multiple concurring diseases including chronic fatigue syndrome, depression (six times more than the general population), autoimmune disease, heart disease, irritable bowel syndrome, obesity, and gastroesophageal reflux disease.

Chronic marital stress is traumatic. It is an example of type 2 trauma, and it is reasonable to conclude that it can be associated with the development of complex PTSD. My patients who are "surviving" chronic marital stress are not doing well, medically speaking, but are often unaware of the source of their symptoms. They come to my office with many of the conditions previously noted, and they're looking for a physical reason for their symptoms, having no insight into the very real possibility that their toxic marriage may be the root source of their medical problems.

One reason patients find it hard to understand that their symptoms might be stress-induced is because they are not "feeling stressed" at that time.

Everybody knows what it feels like to be "stressed." They might experience muscle tension, tremulousness, palpitations, or sweating. This is relatively easy to identify. If their physical symptoms corresponded to an obvious stressful source, they would not be in my office. They would have made the connection themselves and tried to alleviate their stress in some way.

But what if we have symptoms of stress without any obviously identifying source? That is where the confusion sets in. Dr. van der Kolk says,

> Almost every brain-imaging study of trauma patients finds
> abnormal activation of the insula. The insula can transmit

signals to the amygdala that trigger fight/flight responses. This does not require any cognitive input or any conscious recognition that something has gone awry—you just feel on edge and unable to focus or, at worst, have a sense of imminent doom. These powerful feelings are generated deep inside the brain and cannot be eliminated by reason or understanding.[5]

If it is possible (and I think it is) to experience the physiologic effects of stress without being cognitively aware of the source of that stress, then wouldn't it stand to reason that we would likely suffer many of the physical symptoms of chronic stress without being aware of our stressor? I believe this is happening to many people, many of whom are women involved in abusive relationships. We need to help identify the source of the symptoms and help lead people to a healthier, and much happier, life.

Reversing the Vicious Cycle

It would be easy at this point for a mate to become disillusioned with Julie and others who feel overwhelmed with stress, post-traumatic stress, and especially complex post-traumatic stress. It is hard to know how to help them, since their stress is so overwhelming. They are discouraged with their lives, and their discouragement can be contagious.

We can't allow ourselves to grow discouraged.

As doctors, we must seek to reinforce the smallest efforts at growth, change, and ultimately, self-confidence. We must fight for those who struggle to fight for themselves. We must encourage those who are discouraged.

The situation is not hopeless. Fortunately, self-confidence is not built entirely on circumstances. Self-confidence is not completely dependent on what is happening externally, but rather on attitude. We can find small victories in life and build upon them. We can find small areas of life we can control and expand on them.

Victor Frankl, an Austrian psychiatrist, showed us that attitude meant everything in the face of unimaginable stress and hopelessness.

In his book *Man's Search for Meaning,* Frankl shared how he discovered meaning in his suffering as he faced the horror of death in Nazi concentration camps, including Auschwitz.

Frankl taught us that our circumstances need not dictate our attitude. In fact, we can choose how we will face adversity. He discovered we can overcome adversity if we find meaning in our struggle. In this way we open our minds to new possibilities, seeking answers we previously thought impossible. We can even find joy in the midst of our suffering.

Even in your darkest hours of horrible stress and feelings of hopelessness, you have inner resources. You have a faith walk that can support and restore you.

You can believe the words of the psalmist:

> Even though I walk through the darkest valley, I will fear no evil, for you are with me; your rod and your staff, they comfort me. You prepare a table before me in the presence of my enemies. You anoint my head with oil; my cup overflows (Psalm 23:4-5).

These are not simply feel-good words; they are truths we can cling to. They are principles we can grab hold of until our feelings follow.

Braced with these biblical truths, we can find hope in the most troubling situation. We can put one foot in front of the other as we remain actively involved in our lives. We can face challenges head-on and recover from our overwhelming stress by setting healthy boundaries and tending to our personal hygiene, sleep, exercise, and eating habits. Small step by small step, with support on each side, we can turn a vicious cycle around.

Small Steps Matter

Sometimes we become too attached to our problems. We become obsessed with how we are feeling or what is happening to us physically. It's easy to do.

Small steps in the right direction matter. Sometimes we need to step back from our feelings of overwhelming, crazy stress and imagine not being defined by our problems. Imagine our problems teaching us something, much like Dr. Frankl did in those concentration camps. He asked questions about his suffering, looking for meaning in every situation—and he found it.

Julie can find meaning in her situation too. She might step back from her anger at Sam and decode her problems, determining what she can change and what she has little power to change. (We have more ability to impact our lives than we realize.)

Julie confronted Sam and challenged him to go to their friends and un-scapegoat her. This took significant courage on her part and energy she thought she did not have. Still, she pressed forward. In doing so she gained courage, strength, and confidence.

Self-confidence begets self-confidence, which begets more self-confidence. It's viral; and once it's started, it's hard to stop.

Small steps matter.

The Path Forward

Much of what you have heard and believed about stress is wrong or incomplete. While some forms of stress are quite benign, and in fact helpful to getting a job done, other forms of stress can severely harm us.

Some forms of stress, like complex post-traumatic stress, are utterly debilitating and will take great care to overcome. With the right attitude and attention, you can overcome and become a healthy, functioning adult again.

While you cannot always choose your circumstances, remember you are always able to choose your attitude. As Dr. Frankl showed us, meaning can be found in our most troubling situation; and, as we find meaning, we find strength and joy.

Let's now continue our journey toward understanding the true impact of interpersonal conflict on your life.

SIX

EXHAUSTION AND THE EMOTIONAL HANGOVER

After that, you are so emotionally and physically drained, you just go to sleep.

—CEDRIC BOZEMAN

I'd never felt so humiliated and ashamed.

It was five years ago, more or less. My wife and I had had a fight, largely of my own making. I started it because I was tired. Maybe I was utterly exhausted and she did something that irritated me.

That doesn't matter.

What does matter is that I fought with my wife, Christie. Not just a fight, but an emotional eruption. I remember her standing frozen in disbelief as I yelled at her. I don't really want to think about it again. I want to blot it out of my memory, but it happened.

I yelled at her and asked her to leave. She remained frozen, saying a few things to try to calm me down. I was angry about something and was going to speak my mind. And I did.

Finally, I stormed off. She packed a bag and left.

Soon I realized, to a certain extent, the damage I had done. I didn't want her to leave. Far from it. I didn't want to be away from her. I didn't want brokenness in our marriage.

But it was too late for that. Christie now needed space from me, and she deserved it. I gave her the space and settled into self-pity and shame. I had acted in ways that no self-respecting person should act. I said things no self-respecting and wife-respecting person should ever say.

Now I would wait and hope to redeem myself, drained of self-respect and energy, feeling as if I had been hit by a bus and certain Christie felt the same, if not worse.

Several hours later Christie graciously allowed me to apologize. But no apology or pledge to "take back what I said" could really take back what I said. Only time and good behavior would remedy the problem. For now, we could only cope with the event and set our minds on the future.

Emotional Hangover

Fortunately, an event like that has never recurred. But what if events like this were habitual? What if you endured this kind of relationship stress on a daily basis? If you do, surely you're drained of precious energy, hope, and clarity.

Only so much energy is given to us on a daily basis, and each emotional struggle saps that precious energy, leaving us with the dreaded emotional hangover.

You know this feeling. Having had a fight, large or small, you settle into post-fight confusion and exhaustion. Depleted of energy and clarity, you ponder how the fight happened, asking, *Why did it happen? How do I ensure it never happens again? How do we ensure these conflicts don't happen again?*

Sadly, you rarely experience clarity in this space. After all, your brain is overloaded, muddled in confusion. You've had so much adrenaline and cortisol surging through your veins and into your brain, you cannot possibly think straight.

Perpetual relationship stress is sure to cause emotional hangovers. You struggle and struggle with little relief. The constant fights take the life, energy, and physical stamina out of you.

Little is written about emotional hangovers. Of course, we know about hangovers from alcohol, and there is little difference.

Let's compare the symptoms of a hangover from a fight versus a hangover from drinking.

- Emotional hangovers leave you exhausted from the

ongoing conflict; alcohol hangovers also leave you fatigued and weak.

- Emotional hangovers cause confusion about how and why the conflict continues; alcohol hangovers cause dizziness.

- Emotional hangovers create anger at yourself and your mate for the conflict; alcohol hangovers create increased sensitivity to stress and overreactions.

- Emotional hangovers create confusion about your part in the conflict; alcohol hangovers create a loss of judgment and insight.

- Emotional hangovers create shame about engaging in the conflict; alcohol hangovers also create shame about drinking and behavior.

- Emotional hangovers make us feel physically ill and depleted; alcohol hangovers lead to vomiting, headaches, and stomach pain.

- Emotional hangovers lead to depression and hopelessness; alcohol hangovers also lead to depression and hopelessness.

You can certainly see just how horrible this condition is. It is a stress that is not simply stress. It is debilitating, mind-numbing, body-depleting sickness—a hangover for which there is no easy cure.

Exhausted and Ashamed

It is one thing to feel exhausted. It is quite another to feel exhausted and ashamed. Whether you were the victim of emotional abuse or the perpetrator of conflict, your emotional hangover comes with a particularly harmful side effect: Shame.

Shame is a common topic among psychologists, for they know that shame is particularly debilitating. Shame robs us of emotional vitality and physical health. Shame steals our joy. Shame sinks into our souls and pummels us with pervasive feelings of worthlessness.

Shame is often divided into two categories: *Healthy shame* and *toxic shame.* Healthy shame is the temporary feeling of remorse for some behavior that goes against our beliefs and values. Your parents undoubtedly told you that you should feel ashamed of those actions and may well have been right. Healthy shame is that voice that says we have acted against what we know to be right and true. We have violated our conscience and now our conscience reminds us of it.

Thankfully, this fleeting feeling dissipates. We can diminish feelings of shame by taking responsibility for our wrongful, hurtful actions and making amends to the wounded one. We can usually make things right when it comes to healthy shame.

Then there is toxic shame.

Toxic shame is not only feeling as if we have done something bad, but that we *are* bad. Toxic shame sticks to us, seeping into our very bones.

Scott Peck, author of *The Road Less Travelled,* was one of the first to identify this debilitating condition. Quoting Peck, counselor John Bradshaw shared that we all have a smattering of neurotic and character disordered traits, but the hallmark of emotional health "requires the willingness and the capacity to suffer continual self-examination." Bradshaw continued, "Such an ability requires a good relationship to oneself. This is precisely what no shame-based person has. In fact, a toxically shamed person has an adversarial relationship with him/herself. Toxic shame—the shame that binds us—is the basis for both neurotic and character disordered syndromes of behavior."[1]

This is quite a statement. Toxic shame, according to Bradshaw, is at the root of most emotional and many physical maladies. I agree. An emotional hangover is fueled by toxic shame—and lots of it.

For days after my fight with Christie I felt terrible, emotionally and physically. I felt restless, wanting to run but with no place to go. I wanted to hide, but there was no place to hide from myself. Thankfully my shame was a healthy shame and gave me motivation to never repeat that behavior.

Toxic shame would have been much worse. What if I couldn't let go of feeling bad? What if my feelings of shame turned into feelings of chronic inadequacy?

Remember that relationship stress fuels toxic shame. They join and reinforce each other.

We are dependent on rest and relaxation to rejuvenate us, and yet relationship stress robs us of that possibility. We are too tired to fight our haunting conscience that says we are bad and deserve to be punished.

Caroline

Caroline was the first to introduce me to the notion of an emotional hangover. At 35, she was younger than most women seeking counseling from me.

"I used to have a very successful business," she said. "Now I can't run my graphic design business and take care of our two children. I feel like I'm emotionally hungover."

Unfamiliar with the term, I asked for clarification.

"I can't shake the feelings of exhaustion and confusion," she said. "I rarely feel fully alive and alert. I'm always reeling from something my husband, Brad, has done. He always puts me off guard."

"Yes," I said. "But why do you call it an emotional hangover?"

"Because that's the only way I know to describe it," she said. "It's like drinking too much like I was in college. I feel groggy. It is far worse than tired. It is really exhaustion. I could take a nap ten times a day if I didn't have children to care for, but I have to be there for them."

Caroline continued.

"I don't think you understand," she said. "This is far worse than just being tired. I'd love to just feel tired. This is being so tired I cannot think straight."

"And you believe it's tied to conflict with Brad?" I asked.

"Absolutely," she said. "When I get away from him for a couple of days I always feel better. So imagine how I feel when I think that it's my husband making me sick? I feel terrible. I feel ashamed of myself. No Christian wife should feel that way toward her husband."

Caroline was in an incredibly difficult place. I had no easy answers for her and wondered how I could help.

Emotional Quicksand

"Let's talk more specifically about what happens that makes you exhausted," I said.

"Okay," she responded quickly. "I'll tell you about what happened this morning.

"Just before coming to this appointment I asked Brad if he could help me get the kids ready to take to our babysitter. You'd think I was asking him to move a mountain for me. I asked him nicely to help me, but he got all riled up and criticized me for not planning ahead. He scolded me for not being more prepared. He told me I hadn't considered that he had important things to do, and I wasn't holding up my end of our family responsibilities. I was putting him out. I argued with him, which I hate, and finally told him to forget it, that I would take care of everything, like usual."

"Your husband sounds very entitled," I said.

"Absolutely," she said sharply. "If I ask for help he gets angry with me. Then when he gets angry, I get sucked into a fight with him."

"That's where I think we can do some work, Caroline," I said. "While it may be very hard to do, you can work at not getting sucked in. We may have to work on setting boundaries as well."

"I know that is where I need to do work," she said. "He can provoke me into arguing, and then I pay for it for days."

"Pay for it?" I asked.

"Emotional hangover," she said. "I play the fight over and over in my head until I nearly drive myself crazy. I play back his criticism, wondering if there is truth in what he's saying."

"That sounds like emotional quicksand," I said. "Once you get hooked, you're going to get pulled into a battle. After you're pulled in, you're going to sink. Can you see that?"

"It reminds me of what my mom used to tell me about detachment," she said. "I think she learned it in Al-Anon. You've got to know when to try to make a point and when to pull back and detach."

"That's perfectly right, Caroline," I said. "It is up to each of us to know when a conversation is going well and is healthy, as opposed to when it is going to pull us down into quicksand. It's not always easy to make that decision and certainly isn't easy to know when to set a limit."

"It's also not easy to know what I should be able to ask for," she said, "and what to simply leave alone."

I could more clearly see how her relationship stress was causing exhaustion and an emotional hangover.

"It's Not Who I Am"

Caroline continued sharing stories like the ones I've heard from countless others who have struggled with chronic relationship stress, marked by a sense that they are living someone else's life. They have a sense that because of the chronic, unending stress they are detached from the person they know themselves to be.

"This is not supposed to be my life," Caroline said, beginning to cry. "I'm a creative person, a graphic designer. I want to be designing and helping people put their dreams out into the world, and now I can't do that. This is not who I am."

I sat quietly with Caroline as she cried. She was grieving a life she had had—her life. She was grieving the life that was now hers, one filled with exhaustion and emotional hangovers.

"Have you seen my website?" she asked.

"No," I said. "What is it? Are you still working with it?"

"No, I don't do it anymore," she said slowly. "But I used to help people create beautiful logos and print materials for their businesses. My website shows what I was doing, but I'm not taking on any clients. Right now I can't focus enough to really do a good job for anyone. My website feels like a cemetery holding the bones of who I was."

I felt very sad for Caroline. Indeed, she had lost her life. Endless emotional hangovers and exhaustion had stolen her joy.

"I think there is a way to recapture your old life, Caroline," I said. "Would you like my help to recover your old self?"

I hoped my words did not seem hollow. I wanted to help her and knew that her life, her love, was in the person she had lost. I needed to think about how best to help her along this journey.

Depersonalization

Caroline was not living her life. While many of us can identify with her loss of a dream, her loss is deeper and more severe than most. Caroline may be suffering from what has been called *depersonalization*—an "out of body" experience that is a severe reaction to ongoing, complex post-traumatic stress.

As you've learned, chronic stress takes a huge toll. When one loses hope of anything changing, their stress can lead to post-traumatic stress, which can culminate in complex post-traumatic stress. Under these conditions it is not unusual for a person to so severely detach from current stressors that they become depersonalized.

"Sometimes I feel completely detached from my body," Caroline shared. "But not always. When I feel detached I feel like I'm looking down at someone else's life. I wonder, who is this person who is so tired, weak, and lifeless? Where am I—the person I want to be?"

Many experiencing ongoing, chronic relationship stress seek desperate measures to cope, such as depersonalizing. Depersonalization is an altered state of self-awareness and identity that results in feeling separated from oneself. It is a sense of experiencing your own thoughts, behavior, and feelings from a dreamlike distance. It is like watching your life from a distance, as if you were actually watching your life as opposed to participating in it. It is typically associated with anxiety and depression.

Traci Pedersen, in an article titled "Depersonalization," says, "Depersonalization is a harmless, but often very troubling, mental state characterized by a disruption in one's self-perception and awareness. The sufferer's thoughts, emotions and actions feel detached, unreal or foreign, as if they are not a part of oneself."[2]

Coping Poorly with Relationship Stress

We all have a propensity to cope with, adapt to, and accommodate stress in less than ideal ways. Exhaustion, emotional hangovers, and symptoms of depersonalization are only a few of the ways we experience serious relationship stress. These are more ways we cope poorly with severe relationship stressors:

- *Anxiety.* This can be experienced as jittery feelings, heart palpitations, or even anxiety attacks, which manifest in many ways and can be very frightening.

- *Isolation.* Some people pull away from others, withdrawing from friendships and sometimes, more rarely, even reaching a point of being fearful of going out (agoraphobia).

- *Abusing alcohol or drugs.* Excessive use of alcohol or drugs may seem to be a temporary solution, but ultimately causes even more problems.

- *Cutting, picking at, or burning yourself.* This is an extremely harmful way to attempt to cope with anxiety and stress.

- *Engaging in unsafe sexual activities.* With exhaustion often comes loss of impulse control, loss of judgment, and making poor decisions in an effort to find relief.

- *Avoiding dealing with problems.* Denial is powerful, and we may attempt to fool ourselves into thinking we are coping with stress when we are really avoiding solving problems.

- *Using food to soothe troubled feelings.*

- *Attempting suicide.* This is, of course, a drastic measure in an attempt to alleviate inner emotional pain.

- *Surrendering to your pain in resignation.* Here you decide there is nothing you can do but to live the life you have, filled with pain and misery.

- *Avoiding pleasant activities.* You withdraw from healthy social events, exercise, and friendships.

If you use any of the above measures to cope with relationship stress, you must seek professional help. Each of the above actions is a way to avoid experiencing and facing emotional and relationship stress, and each one leads to even greater problems such as alcoholism or drug addiction, eating disorders, depression, and debilitating anxiety.

A Necessary Separation

What might it take for Caroline to regain her life? How might she be able to wake up and reclaim it?

Often restabilizing your life requires separation from the ongoing, debilitating relationship stress. While no one wants to take such drastic measures, and I don't like to recommend a marital separation, it is sometimes necessary to regain some sense of emotional equilibrium.

Think about it. If you face daily relationship stress, as opposed to daily relationship joy, you need relief. If you find yourself coping in unhealthy ways, you need the relief that can occur from making healthy choices. You need relief from the cortisol bombardment that occurs with constant stress. Unfortunately, this relief sometimes comes only with a separation from a troubled relationship.

Sadly, many wait too long to take this needed break from stress. In an effort to give their marriage every opportunity at success they actually deplete their emotional and energy reserves and do themselves, and their marriage, harm.

Too many "blow apart" rather than take a reasoned approach to navigating a time away from each other. They wait until they have another huge fight and then, completely discouraged, separate as a last-ditch effort to save their relationship.

Recently I recommended separation for a couple who had counseled with me for some time. After a roller coaster of highs and lows, they really hadn't made much progress. They were mired in a pattern of bickering that had marked their 20-year marriage, and our counseling had failed to alter these entrenched patterns. She blamed him while he blamed her, and the truth was, they were both responsible. Nonetheless, the more emotionally frazzled they became, the less productive they were at resolving their relationship issues. A separation helped them regain emotional stamina so they could work more effectively on their marriage.

This was also the case for Caroline. She, too, had spent her emotional reserves and needed a break to clear her mind and determine a path forward. Separation is never an easy decision, but it is sometimes a necessary one.

Regaining Energy

We all have limited energy, and it is our responsibility to manage it. We must know what gives us energy and what steals it from us.

Psychologist Adele Ryan McDowell, in her article "5 Ways to Deal with an Emotional Hangover," writes, "As a result of some emotionally incendiary experience where you feel wronged, not valued, misunderstood, or crossed, you can find yourself on one wild ride of emotions. You spin round and round and round, until eventually you are spent."[3]

Fortunately, just as sure as you can lose your emotional sobriety and subsequently physical health, you can regain your limited supply of energy. It will, however, require diligence and effort, as well as the following steps.

1. *Get emotional support.* Friendships mitigate stress. Researchers have long known that those surrounded by loved ones fare better than those who are isolated. Are you sharing your stress with those able to support, love, and care for you?

2. *Externalize your emotional and physical pain.* We often "carry" our pain, and fortunately, we can externalize it as well. This is possible through activities like exercise, yoga, and certain meditation practices. Monitoring your emotions, noting them, and then allowing them to pass is another way to externalize emotional pain. Do you have daily practices that mitigate your pain?

3. *Set your boundaries.* We must recognize the origins of our relationship stress. While we may be tempted to blame some other person, our stress may be multiplied by our refusal to say yes or no to others' actions in our lives. Spend time with your emotional distress and ask yourself if there is some boundary you need to set to limit stress coming into your life. Where do you need to set firmer boundaries?

4. *Embrace change.* Most of us are creatures of habit, doing things the way we've always done them. Unfortunately, this doesn't serve us well. You've probably heard that doing the same things and expecting different results is the definition of insanity. Are you looking for new information? Are you willing to take a risk and try something new and healthier for your life?

5. *Prepare for the challenges that come with change.* Change is rarely easy, though it is often good for us. Change demands that we be prepared for the concomitant challenges. Change rocks our world, shaking the foundation of a world we may be firmly attached to, even if that world is bad for us. Change then opens us to new possibilities and new energy. Do you mentally and physically prepare for change?

6. *Determine other ways of caring for yourself.* If you reflect upon your life, you may discover you have many inner resources you have never tapped into. Sitting quietly in your favorite places can give you new insights. Ask yourself questions such as, "What does this challenge ask of me?" and "What changes am I afraid of facing?"

7. *Be patient with yourself.* Finally, be patient with yourself. Change is never easy, and results rarely come quickly. But growth comes to those willing to embrace the journey. Trust that God will finish the good work He has started in you. Do you trust God with your changes?

From a Physician: Dr. Joshua Hawkins, Surgeon

"Dear God, we thank You for the life of patient X," was how we began every operation in Burundi, East Africa. Two years ago, I spent two weeks in a rural African hospital relieving a full-time American surgeon away on furlough in the United States. It was an overtly evangelical medical practice. We prayed with every patient.

At the start of every surgery, the anesthetist would lead the prayer. Simple. Heartfelt. They didn't have much. But heartfelt prayer was one thing they had.

After 36 hours of traveling, I was met by my partner from my practice back home, who had been there the preceding two weeks. He was waiting at the gate of the medical compound, ready to escort me to the operating suite. A difficult case had come up during his time there, and he managed to stall until the day I arrived so we could take advantage of 12 hours of overlap with the two of us to tackle it.

In Africa, surgery is often the end of the line for every medical illness. With standard medicines and technologies in critical shortage or completely unavailable, diseases progress until they either can be cured by surgery or become fatal. A two-year-old child had been brought in with a newly diagnosed abdominal mass. We had no CT scan, only a simple ultrasound machine. The ultrasound showed a large tumor arising from the kidney. No pathology would be available to sort it out. The child could not be flown to a place with sophisticated care. The diagnosis was almost certainly Wilms tumor. While this was serious at home, here it was lethal unless it could be safely removed with surgery. In a small child this is a very dangerous operation. We had to try.

I dropped my bags, wolfed down some food and coffee, and staggered across the dusty dirt road into the poorly equipped operating suite. Eight hours later, after many tenuous moments, my partner and I exchanged high-fives across the patient. The tumor was out. We began the process of closing the abdomen. Minutes later we received the crushing news across the drapes: The patient had no pulse, and hadn't for many minutes. We learned later the anesthesia provider was a Burundian doctor having only a few months of experience with anesthesia, and none putting a breathing tube into a child for surgery like this. The child hadn't gotten oxygen for many minutes, and now had no signs of life. After a few more futile minutes trying to resuscitate him, he was pronounced dead.

We shared the agonizing news with the child's mother. Her first words will ring in my heart forever: "Thank you for trying." And then we cried. It still hurts now.

I have had to share similarly devastating news with families here at home hundreds of times. And not once has the initial response been so staggeringly understanding.

I work for a public hospital. Which means that if I spent my time praying with patients and families who weren't asking for it, I wouldn't have a job. One amazing thing about my job as a surgeon is the intensity. I enter into people's lives at the moment of their greatest weakness, vulnerable and dependent on God. What I do is so incredibly mind-blowing that I am constantly aware of my own fallibility and complete reliance on God.

I pray every day that God would heal my patients and that He would give me wisdom and judgment and humility. Many patients experience incredible healing. But some patients die of their diseases, some suffer terrible complications, and all feel alone and yearn for answers from a God who feels far away when things seem to be going poorly. While I don't ascribe to a prosperity gospel theology, I do believe that it is good to ask God to heal us of our physical diseases. I have committed my entire professional career to being His instrument to do just that. God does not want us to suffer from our diseases. As a surgeon, my chief aim is to bring God glory. Sometimes I will do that by skillfully eradicating cancer in humility. Sometimes He will do that in spite of me, but not through means that make sense to me or my patients.

In John 16:33, Jesus says, "In the world you will have tribulation. But take heart; I have overcome the world" (ESV). Being upset at God because of medical illness does not weaken our faith. Disease should be heartbreaking.

Seeking and Regaining Clarity

I love writing, reflecting, and praying in the morning. Sitting quietly in my office, I'm able to think clearly while the house slowly awakens and invites in the new day. In this sacred space, decorated and designed specifically for me, I care for myself. I feel renewed and alive.

In the evening, I also anticipate the following day, knowing I will regain clarity and energy that has ebbed as the day draws to a close. I know that in this particular moment I may be tired, but a good night's sleep will help me regain clarity.

It's possible that you aren't able to gain clarity from something as simple as a good night's sleep. In fact, sleep may be a challenge due to the relationship stress you experience. Nonetheless, you must seek and regain clarity and know what will bring it to you.

We must all seek clarity. Whether it is through a marital separation, some or all of the practices I use, or something as simple as a good night's sleep, clarity is not something that happens to us, but rather something we cultivate.

If you are intentional about obtaining clarity and renewed energy in your life, it can be yours; but you must be keenly tuned into your life, knowing your needs and attending to them.

It's Your Health

Having a healthy life ultimately means taking full responsibility for it. As much as I believe in the medical and psychological professions, I know no doctor is going to care for you better than you care for yourself.

It's your health, and you must ultimately take responsibility for it!

You cannot take responsibility for your relational, emotional, and physical health if you are not awake and alive to your life.

What do I mean by this?

Much has been written about being present in your life. This may seem like an odd topic, but the concept is critical to having a healthy life.

What do I mean by being present in your life? I mean the opposite of finding ways to anesthetize yourself to your current pain. Whether you use any of the destructive coping mechanisms listed earlier, denying your pain, or simply busying yourself, you must come alive. You must attend to your life.

What would you do if a friend approached you in distress? Imagine the following 911 call from your best friend:

> Hello. I'm sorry to bother you. I'm in trouble. My husband had another rage reaction scaring us to death. He's been yelling and threatening me. The kids heard everything. He wouldn't stop. I grabbed the kids and left. I'm not sure what to do. I really hate to bother you. Can you help?

What would you do? Of course you would drop everything to help. Everything you had going on would recede into the background as the urgency of the present situation took focus. You would make emotional and physical space for your friend. You would create a safe place for her and her children. You would nurture and comfort her.

I'm now asking you to do that for yourself. Are you any less deserving of comfort and compassion than your best friend? No!

Sadly, we are often more compassionate with others than we are with ourselves. As much as we may tout caring for ourselves, we often simply do not. We are often harried, hurried, tired, and frayed with anxiety. We neglect ourselves and ask our doctors to fix our troubled psyches and bodies.

Such an attitude will not bring healing.

So I ask you to show up for your life and take responsibility for your well-being. Be present, pay attention, and listen carefully to your friend—your Self. I ask you to pay attention, stop coping destructively, and tend to your health.

What do you need? A physical separation from your mate? A weekend away? More quiet mornings with your journal? More time to pray and consider your situation? God promises to give wisdom generously to those who seek it (James 1:5).

The Path Forward

Just like an alcohol hangover, an emotional hangover can leave us reeling and dazed. No less troublesome, an emotional hangover is a warning to us that we are losing our life.

Regaining your emotional, physical, and relational health takes focus and intentionality. Are you ready for change? You must let go of the life you've been clinging to. Your old life won't serve you well. It's time for change. Are you ready? Strap on your parachute and get ready to jump.

Let's now continue our journey toward understanding the true impact of relationship stress on your life by looking more closely at toxic anger.

Seven

The Anger That Fuels Everything

*I really believe that all of us have a lot of darkness
in our souls. Anger, rage, fear, and sadness. I
don't think that's reserved for people who have
horrible upbringings. I think it really exists and is
part of the human condition. I think in the course
of your life you figure out ways to deal with that.*

—KEVIN BACON

"I can't believe how I acted," Rebecca said to me in an urgent phone call. I'd counseled her over the phone a couple of times before.

"I just snapped," she continued, her frustration obvious. "My husband stared at me in disbelief, obviously shocked at my outburst. It wasn't like me, but I couldn't help myself."

I asked more questions.

"What do you mean when you say you snapped?" Sure, I'd heard and understood this term, but I needed Rebecca to explain what it meant to her.

"I yelled at my husband," she said. "I called him rude and insensitive. I don't know what else I said, but it wasn't good."

"Tell me more about what was going on," I said. "What was happening just before you snapped?"

"Not that much," she said. "My brother and sister-in-law were in the room too, and I'm just so embarrassed. This is not like me."

"I hear you," I said, "but let's try to understand why you blurted out what you did. You didn't react out of nothing. It sounds like you were being mistreated."

I wanted to understand the context of her angry outburst.

"Our marriage is awful," Rebecca said. "Sam treats me with contempt. I said something and he rolled his eyes at me and then laughed at what I was saying. I just yelled at him. He talks to me the way my parents talk to me and the way my brother talks to me. I hate it. But I usually can hold it in."

"Did he hurt your feelings?" I asked.

"He hurts my feelings all the time," she said sharply. "My brother typically sticks up for him, and my sister-in-law is like me. She does nothing. Her marriage is probably the same as mine. She's probably in the same boat."

"What do you mean?" I asked.

"My brother is mean, like my husband," she said. "My brother turned out just like my dad. He treats me and my sister rudely, and his wife is like me. But I usually don't react. I usually pretend I didn't see his actions or hear his words. But this time I couldn't hold back my words. I told my husband he was mean and then walked out of the room. I never do that."

"What do you normally do?" I asked.

"I'm not sure," she said. "I kind of pretend not to see it."

Rebecca paused and seemed to reflect further.

"I guess I defend myself a little and then shut down," she said. "It doesn't do any good to stick up for myself. I've never stood up for myself with my family. I've learned not to share my real feelings. I hate the way my dad, brother, and my husband treat me. I guess I'm carrying around anger about it. I don't know."

"That's a good place to begin," I said. "Typically anger is a feeling we have when we feel wronged in some way. Let's talk about that possibility."

I spent more time with Rebecca helping her understand the context of her anger—why she feels what she feels, how she expresses it, and the impact it has on her well-being and her relationships. I told her that her anger sounded justified and there was much she could learn from it. It could become an ally, but she needed to learn why she reacted the way she did.

In this chapter we'll focus on anger—anger that fuels.

Anger Defined

How can we explain what happened to this woman? Her eruption was not typical for her. She shared that she typically stuffed her hurt and finally reacted to a provocation and exploded—completely out of character for her.

This is often the case with anger. Many try to control it, suppressing it until it leaks out. It can come out in an explosive tirade or more indirectly. It has been said if we are passive long enough we will become passive-aggressive, or aggressive. Anger cannot and will not be suppressed indefinitely.

Anger is a natural, adaptive response to a threat of some kind. Anger is an emotional state varying in intensity from mild irritation to intense fury or rage. It ranges from feeling tense to feeling enraged.

Anger begins by feeling threatened in some way, leading to a surge in blood pressure and an increase in energy hormones, adrenaline, and noradrenaline. We are ready to defend ourselves. Our pupils constrict, our muscles tighten, our breathing becomes shallow, and we ready ourselves for combat.

Unfortunately, too often we fail to understand and deal with our anger appropriately, and the result is what happened with Rebecca—she just "snapped." She was surprised by her angry eruption, and her husband and family may have been as well.

In my book *The Power of Emotional Decision Making,* I share the following story about my own father:

> My father would come home in the early evening after a long day at the office and find dishes in the sink. He was obviously displeased about this, expecting the house to be orderly and peaceful. He subsequently spewed anger at my mother and my sisters, ultimately turning his anger onto me for failing to take the garbage out.
>
> "What have you been doing all afternoon? I told you to have those dishes in the sink cleaned when I got home!"
>
> And then he turned on me.
>
> "Why haven't you taken out the garbage, David?"

I'd sputter something, having no good excuse.

"I'll do it, Dad."

"Do it now!"

The unpredictability of my father's eruptions was the most confusing part. Because he was generally a happy and even playful man, his anger frightened me. When I sensed he was in a foul mood, ready to pounce on someone, I'd head for the basement to hide out. I didn't like his anger and most certainly didn't like to be the recipient of it.[1]

Unexpressed Anger

How can we understand Rebecca and my father? Both snapped. Both erupted, much like a volcano erupts with molten lava. Both this woman and my father had a kind of "molten lava" buried within them, and the impact of their suppressed anger on themselves and those around them was destructive.

Anger is generally considered a secondary emotion. When we look deeper, we often find that our molten lava is really hurt, sadness, fear, and other emotions that have not been metabolized. Notice that Rebecca, her husband, her father, her brother, and my father had other feelings they were not dealing with in a healthy manner. Again, this emotion must go somewhere. That is one reason the body cannot help but contain all this unexpressed tension.

All emotion is helpful and natural, but anger leads us astray very quickly. We know that bottling up emotions is unhealthy. There is much evidence that unexpressed anger can lead to all kinds of physical symptoms, which we will address later in this chapter.

Most of us feel uncomfortable with our anger. We might have a sense we are carrying around some molten lava, and we seek ways to suppress it. But anger, like most emotions, is *e-motion*, energy in motion. You cannot simply suppress it. You cannot wish it away, but you can pretend it isn't there and doesn't exist.

Unexpressed anger, however, creates all kinds of problems and leaks out in indirect ways. It can lead to pathological expressions of anger such as the following:

- *Passive-aggressive behavior.* We find ways to get even with those we carry grudges against. We might avoid them, withdrawing from them, or find ways of not supporting them. We may "forget" to do something they have asked of us.

- *Sarcasm.* Sarcasm has been called anger in a clown suit. Sarcasm is derisive and hurtful, always concealing inner turmoil and tension.

- *Physical tirades.* Sooner or later anger erupts. Anger eruptions may take the form of slamming doors, throwing things, or stomping around.

- *Verbal tirades.* Molten, eruptive anger may take the form of a temper tantrum, spewing forth of verbal accusations. The verbal tirade may include name-calling, threats, and ultimatums.

- *Sulking.* Withdrawing from our mate, we punish them with our silence, all the while justifying our right to do so. The "silent treatment" is a particularly lethal form of passive aggression.

- *Cynicism.* Carrying around the molten lava for a period of time leads to a cynical spirit. We tend to be negative and critical of others, and this sour attitude impacts everyone in our world.

- *Criticizing everything.* Closely related to cynicism, harboring anger often leads to being critical about little things. We become perfectionistic and watch for others failing to live up to our standards, so we can point it out.

Can you imagine how these behaviors wreak havoc on us both emotionally and with potential physical side effects? This list of behaviors causes untold impact on the body and mind. One cannot have adrenaline surging through the body on a chronic basis without it taking an enormous toll. Remember the emotional hangover discussed in the last chapter?

Toxic Anger

There is a difference between anger, the kind we all experience from time to time, and toxic anger, which lingers internally and is corrosive to ourselves and others. Anger felt and expressed in a respectful way can be useful; but toxic, vitriolic anger hurts everyone. Toxic anger is often a major component of relationship stress—as in the case of Rebecca.

Remember, Rebecca had felt disrespected and dismissed by her father, brother, and husband for years. This fueled her suppressed anger. Ultimately feeling provoked by her husband, she exploded. The anger she carries is the result of being victimized by relationship stress from her husband, brother, and father.

Dr. Jennice Vilhauer writes, "While anger is a normal emotion that when expressed appropriately can facilitate communication and understanding in a relationship, being on the receiving end of someone else's out of control anger can be a very distressing experience that shuts down healthy communication."[2]

My father had toxic anger. Why do I say that? Because my mother, my siblings, and I tiptoed around him at times. Dr. Vilhauer continues, "When people don't trust your emotional responses, and feel they are always walking around on egg shells in your presence, they will change their behavior as a way to prevent triggering your anger. They stop communicating honestly and won't tell you things that they fear may upset you. This results in a loss of authenticity in the relationship."

Rebecca's husband also seems to have toxic anger. Not only does Rebecca tiptoe around him, but she also harbors her own anger. His seems to be explosive while she is implosive. Both are very damaging.

Impact of Toxic Anger

Anger has a horrific impact on our bodies and our emotional well-being. Certainly this is why Scripture says so much about anger. The apostle Paul says that when (not if) we become angry, we should not sin (Ephesians 4:26).

The apostle James says, "You must all be quick to listen, slow to speak, and slow to get angry" (James 1:19 NLT).

Toxic anger—the kind of anger that causes others to shrink and tiptoe around you—is horrifically damaging to everyone's well-being. Toxic anger negatively impacts the body and the mind. Relationships cannot thrive in the midst of toxic anger. Let's consider the emotional impact of living with toxic anger.

The predominant result of toxic anger is fear. Those who live with a toxically angry person have little choice but to shrink in the face of such anger. Fearing reprisal, many in severe relationship stress become smaller and smaller, less and less authentic. To be real means to face scrutiny, criticism, and shame. It becomes easier to slowly withdraw and bury deeper feelings of insecurity and distrust, and the relationship becomes less dynamic.

Rebecca walks on eggshells around her husband, brother, and father. She stifles her anger and occasionally snaps, surprising even herself with her feelings. Tragically, not only does Rebecca live in fear, but she is a ticking time bomb, for she cannot suppress her anger indefinitely. If she cannot express her hurt and emotional distress directly and safely, she will push her feelings down until she snaps again.

She is surprised by her reactions. But when we hear her story we can well imagine that she has underlying feelings of sadness, insecurity, fear, abandonment, and neglect. She cannot, however, share any of those feelings, whether she understands them or not. Subsequently, all these feelings are suppressed and become fuel for her emotional and physical distress.

What is this doing to Rebecca's marriage? Rebecca begins to emotionally divorce her husband one emotional wound at a time. She carries fear and hurt in her body as she also pushes away from her brother, sister-in-law, and parents. Her marriage becomes less and less viable, and her emotional and physical health decline.

All this toxicity takes a huge toll on a person.

In her article "Anger: A Toxic Emotion That May Be Killing You," Diana Anderson-Tyler indicates dangers anger presents to our bodies, including:

1. *Increased risk of heart disease.* Anderson-Tyler cites 44 studies published in the *Journal of the American College of*

Cardiology that found evidence of a link between emotions and heart disease. Scientists speculate that stress hormones activated by anger, such as adrenaline and cortisol, speed up your heart rate and breathing and cause your blood pressure to rise and blood vessels to constrict.

2. *Damage to the liver and kidneys.* Anderson-Tyler notes that the frontal lobe of our brains serves an important role in controlling rage. If you're continuously provoked by anger-inducing triggers, this state of response can begin to cause a decrease in the production of acetylcholine, a hormone that tempers the severe side effect of adrenaline, weakening the heart, stiffening arteries, and causing liver damage.

3. *Slowing in the body's healing process.* Studies show that individuals who have trouble controlling their anger were four times more likely to need more time to heal wounds, compared to those who mastered their anger.[3]

You can see that anger has a powerful impact on our bodies and our emotions. It destroys our bodies and equally destroys our relationships. Only under the most cautious circumstances can it be an emotion used for good.

Anatomy of an Angry Man

Todd is an angry man. Actually, truth be told, Todd is a sad, hurt, fearful man. He modeled himself after his angry father, who learned how to be angry from his father. In Todd's family, anger has been a way of dealing with painful feelings for generations.

Todd was referred to me by his wife, as is often the case for men with anger issues. His wife talked to me briefly prior to my appointment with him, sharing that his anger was a horrible problem. She was considering a separation if he would not seek counsel with me.

A 40-year-old firefighter who had been married for 20 years, he was reluctant to admit his problem and became more defensive when I began probing.

"Look," he began, clearly attempting to take control of our session. "I know what my wife is saying about me, but you don't know the whole story. I'd like to tell you about her first."

"I certainly don't know the whole story, but would like to," I shared. "Can we talk about why she wants you to see me?"

"We can," he said, hesitating. "But that means you've already got your mind made up and there's no point in me even talking."

"Actually, Todd," I said, "I want to talk about her concerns as well as yours. Let's address her concerns first, and I assure you there will be time for you to share your concerns later."

He was not about to give any ground.

"I don't need to say anything," he said sarcastically. "Let's just let her run the show. That's typical. I'm a puppet and I'll just tell you what you want to hear."

Todd's seething anger was thinly veiled. I imagined he was feeling very threatened by the idea of seeing a psychologist. He wanted to present facts in a controlling manner, creating a favorable impression. When that failed, he immediately shifted to playing the victim and attempted to manipulate me, tactics he undoubtedly used with his wife as well.

What was happening inside Todd? Why did he have such a strong need to make a certain impression?

As I've said, anger is most often a secondary emotion, meaning we often resort to anger to protect ourselves from other feelings, and this was certainly true for Todd. Because he didn't know how to feel or talk about other more gentle and vulnerable emotions, anger was the one emotion he felt strangely comfortable in expressing.

Yes, anger, according to most psychologists, is a secondary emotion, if even an emotion. This means that while we call anger an emotion, almost invariably anger covers more vulnerable feelings.

In an article for *Psychology Today,* Dr. Leon Seltzer says, "Those of us who routinely use anger as a 'cover-up' to keep our more vulnerable feelings at bay, generally become so adept at doing so that we have little to no awareness of the dynamic driving our behavior...anger is *the* emotion of invulnerability."[4]

Todd has never learned to identify and discuss his feelings. He has never learned how to assertively share his hurt or sadness, risking making himself more vulnerable in the process. He has only learned to be strong and dominant, a bully. When he is a bully he never has to wrestle with his softer emotions of fear, hurt, and sadness. He feels powerful and strong when he is angry, and he finds that his anger fuels everything in his life.

Anger as a Cry for Help

As destructive as most anger is, it is often a cry for help. Disguised, it is rarely seen for what it is.

I've worked with countless traumatized women who suffer from narcissistic and emotional abuse. In nearly every situation I find women who have experienced what Rebecca experienced—sudden, seemingly inexplicable anger. They have acted like a can of Coke, shaken and opened.

These women don't want to be angry. They are often ashamed, surprised, and embarrassed by the magnitude of their emotion. They don't want to get hooked into fights. They feel out of control, emotionally and relationally. They want help. They want change. They want a troubled situation to be righted.

Their anger is a cry for help, and when we see it as such we can begin to get to the bottom of things.

To be fair, the same can be said for men. Few men really want to be angry. They know no other way to verbalize their pain. As much as any of us may want to push our anger away and deny it exists, something hidden often seeks expression.

On this topic Richard Rohr writes in *Falling Upward*: "Invariably when something upsets you, and you have a strong emotional reaction out of proportion to the moment, your shadow self has just been exposed. So watch for any overreactions or overdenials."[5]

Whether your anger is a cry for help or a cover-up for some other painful feeling or need, the solution is to be gently curious and go on a search for what you really need.

Anger and Repulsion

Anger disguised is very hard to be around. Stephen Hawking wisely said, "People won't have time for you if you are always angry or complaining."[6]

While anger is a natural emotion, it's like TNT and must be handled very carefully. Anger, unrefined and unmanaged, pushes people away. No one wants to be around someone who has anger sitting just below the surface. We all sense, and fear, that anger usually leaks out, often in a most destructive way.

Dr. Harville Hendrix, in his popular book *Getting the Love You Want*, writes that he has witnessed the corrosive impact of anger: "Anger is destructive to a relationship, no matter what its form. When anger is expressed, the person on the receiving end of the attack feels brutalized, whether or not there has been any physical violence."[7]

There is no question that destructive, emotionally abusive relationships create anger and frustration, leading to acting out emotion in indirect ways such as sarcasm, passive-aggressiveness, and sporadic, outward explosion. Subsequently, relationships are further impacted, including our relationship to our Self.

Remember that as we push away from others due to their anger, we push away from opportunities to relate effectively and to grow emotionally. We lose opportunities to feel safe and explore ourselves.

Righteous Indignation and the Gift of Anger

Because anger has so much destructive power, it is not uncommon for us to either suppress it or even outright deny being angry. We must remember that anger is a natural, God-given emotion and can be helpful to our emotional well-being.

Here are a few of the gifts of anger, taken again from my book *The Power of Emotional Decision Making*:

First, *anger can reveal what is important to us*. Our anger typically erupts when something important to us is violated or threatened. Our anger signals that our boundaries have been transgressed in some way. Listening carefully to our anger reveals what is important to us. Our anger often reveals our core values, the truths that make us who we are.

Second, *anger can give us the power to make difficult decisions and carry them out.* Many tolerate injustices for so long and finally, often in a "fit of anger," stand up for themselves. The surge of cortisol and adrenaline becomes the fuel that fires change. When we are faced with a problem that requires more energy, anger helps spur us into action.

Third, *anger defines our boundaries to others.* Anger defines who we are and what is important to us. Anger can make a bold statement to others about what we value and how to relate best to us. We teach people how to treat us, and our anger solidifies our boundaries, sending a strong message about how we expect to be treated.

Fourth, *anger can be used to make important contact with others.* If we are careful about the expression of anger, this emotion can bring us into contact with others in a needful way. We may need to express anger about boundaries that have been violated and clarify what is expected if there is to be an ongoing relationship.

Finally, *anger is a call to action.* Anger is an alert that something needs to change. Our anger is a very strong signal that all is not right in our world. We have been silent for too long, tolerated too much indignity, or settled for a relationship that is not satisfying. Our anger is a blaring signal and a glaring red light indicating a time for change.[8]

Choosing to Be a Peacemaker

I believe we never have to fight. I would say the same is true about anger. I'm not sure we ever have to experience this corrosive emotion, except for those rare occasions when righteous indignation is appropriate.

That is rarely the case.

The apostle James says it like this: "What causes fights and quarrels among you? Don't they come from your desires that battle within you? You desire but do not have, so you kill. You covet but you cannot get what you want, so you quarrel and fight" (James 4:1-2).

James says fighting and anger are rarely completely about someone else, but rather have to do with our own inner attitudes and beliefs. Perhaps we are frustrated with the way things are going, and so we become angry. Perhaps someone violates our flimsy boundaries and we blame them rather than building stronger boundaries.

Both Todd and Rebecca must learn to deal more effectively with their anger. In spite of their histories and current life stories, they can choose to see their anger as a symptom of something else going on inside of them.

The key for Todd and Rebecca, their mates and families, is awareness, insight, and emotion management. Let's explore how this might work.

Terrence Gorski, in his book *Getting Love Right,* writes about dealing effectively with your feelings by following this four-step process:

1. *Recognize your feelings.* Certainly the first step in making progress against anger is to recognize underlying feelings. We have feelings about nearly everything that happens to us in life, and we must become acquainted with those feelings.

2. *Label your feelings.* Our feelings need labels. Anger is not usually anger, but rather unrecognized hurt, sadness, and fear. We must learn to distinguish our feelings.

3. *Affirm your feelings.* Then we must affirm and take ownership of our vulnerable feelings. We can say, "I feel sad about this loss. I feel rejected by my husband." We must embrace our sadness, hurt, and fear. We must draw our hurt close to us and explore the depths of it.

4. *Communicate your feelings.* Finally, we must communicate those feelings. Ideally we are with someone who cares about our feelings and encourages us to express them. Even in the midst of rejection, however, we can affirm our feelings and express them. We can be the champion of our own feelings.[9]

We have the power to follow these steps and transform our relationships. While we cannot change others, we can change how we interact with them; and by doing this, we indirectly change them.

Imagine what might happen if Rebecca became clearer about her feelings, labeled them, affirmed them, and then communicated them.

What if she set strong boundaries with her husband and family, making it clear when and how she would be involved with them? If she made a practice of these steps, I am quite confident she could have a positive impact on her family.

I know you may have doubts about this, and you may be right. Even so, the act of affirming our feelings even in the face of dismissal will have a positive impact on our self-esteem. If we affirm our feelings, cherishing them as if they were vulnerable, young children, we grow in the process. If we add healthy boundaries to the recipe, all the better.

Healing Our Relationships

If anger perpetuates distance and conflict, affirming ourselves and clarifying our feelings to others increases the possibility of connection.

Think about it. Anger creates distance. We cannot draw close to someone who is angry. We draw close to vulnerability. We want to help those who are suffering and wounded, not those who are intimidating.

Fortunately, we can change the way we react and the way we perceive things. Just this morning I helped a couple move from fighting to connection, from anger to hurt and brokenness. This was all done through the power of changing perceptions and being willing to attach themselves to their more vulnerable emotions.

This couple was wounded. They were the epitome of "hurting people hurt people." From their woundedness, they spoke harshly to one another. They voiced that it had taken years to create distance and emotional pain, and now they were very distressed. They came to me in crisis.

When I spoke with them, all they could see and feel was pain. Each had hurt the other, and subsequently they pushed away in self-protection. The very act of pushing away, however, caused each other even more pain. They were caught in a vicious cycle.

Beneath their pain they cared about each other. Like most, they longed to be heard, valued, and appreciated. They were expressing their pain in destructive ways as opposed to ways that would enable them to care for each other's wounds.

Help for them would come from first taking responsibility for the situation they found themselves in. They didn't just land in the middle of their muddle. They made small choice after small choice leading to their emotional demise. Instead of reaching out to each other to help each other heal, they voiced their pain and blamed their mate for it.

Just as their emotional separation came from a series of destructive choices, healing would come from making small, positive choices. They would have to set their pride aside and see that the other was hurting just as much as they were.

I reminded them that the brain is hardwired for fear; the amygdala is triggered by fear, and perceptions become skewed, emotions become overly aroused, and trouble ensues. They have just a quarter of a second to respond instead of react. We have, according to brain research, a quarter of a second to interrupt every fearful or angry urge and disengage from that urge.

While a quarter of a second may not sound like much time, it is enough to interpret perceptions differently. Dan Baker, in his book *What Happy People Know,* says it like this:

> Taking advantage of this quarter-second is somewhat similar to counting to 10 before allowing yourself to become angry. If you've done this, you've probably realized you had more control than you'd thought. But it doesn't take 10 seconds to assert this control. It only takes a fraction of a second.[10]

It is critical that we all practice stepping back from our perception of truth, doubting ourselves, and with humility considering other possibilities. Just as "hurting people hurt people," "healed people heal people."

What if, instead of reacting or snapping, you decided to step back from your emotions? What if you became curious about your reactions to situations, looking within yourself to discover what you are truly feeling and why you are feeling it? This could be a most exciting journey.

From a Physician: Dr. Tyson Hawkins, Internist

Nancy, a 70-year-old married woman, has disabling osteoarthritis in the hands and takes painkillers to make it through the day. She has a hard time sleeping at night and takes sleeping pills. She comes to the office frequently to discuss a variety of concerns ranging from arthritis pain and insomnia to depression, anxiety, and abdominal pain. We have tested blood work on numerous occasions to evaluate for any significant inflammatory cause of her symptoms. It is pretty clear when she is seen, however, that she is suffering from significant stress.

Nancy typically comes in with one or two major complaints, but often spends the majority of her visit discussing her husband. Her husband suffers from a chronic illness which is getting worse. This is taking a toll on Nancy, and subsequently on her health. And it is not just the physical demands that bother her. More than anything she complains that he is becoming angrier. She doesn't know what to do about him.

He is frequently short with her and more demanding of her time. She is taking over all of the household duties, and he does not express any gratitude. She tells me she thinks she is prepared for the increasing physical demands of keeping up the house but is ill prepared to deal with his anger and irritability. She feels trapped by his needs and complaints.

All of this, notably, coincides with increased medical needs and more frequent office visits. I often wonder if she comes just to unload and talk. She feels reassured that she remains in relatively good health without any new significant medical conditions but does not understand why she feels so unwell. She can see that there is a significant stressor in her life but has a harder time making the connection between her physical complaints and her mental anguish.

Nancy is not atypical in any way. She is living with somebody who is angry, and she is dealing with anger of her own regarding her situation.

Not surprisingly, multiple adverse health effects have been linked to anger. Whether it is from the rush of catecholamines and cortisol released during times of anger or from the adverse behaviors we engage in to alleviate our stress (smoking, drinking, high caloric intake), anger has a variety of documented adverse health effects. A meta-analysis published in 2009 showed an association between anger and coronary heart disease (CHD) in both healthy and known CHD populations.[11] Similarly studies show an increased risk of diabetes[12] thought due to both adopting unhealthy dietary habits and to elevated inflammatory markers via activation of the sympathetic nervous system. Harvard University found that in healthy people, simply recalling an angry experience from their past caused a six-hour dip in immunoglobulin A levels.[13] Immunoglobulin A (IgA) serves an important role in the body as our "first line of defense" against infection. This means that angry people may be more susceptible to infection.

In the plentiful research investigating the health risks associated with anger, not surprisingly the conclusion is that it's not good for you! Although I can't identify absolutely which of my patients are dealing with chronic anger, I can tell you which of my patients are seeking medical care more frequently; and I suspect it may have something to do with their emotional status and potentially with unresolved or chronically recurring anger.

Nancy is not an atypical patient. We are working together to help her find a healthier outlet for her frustration, whether it is through support groups, therapy, exercise, or a hobby to get her out of the house for a bit. She, like many caregivers, is becoming increasingly isolated and is feeling the weight of this burden as time goes on.

Love Overcomes Anger

Now we know our anger accomplishes nothing, with the rare exception of righteous indignation. We have learned that most often our anger is fueled by deeper, more vulnerable, and unexpressed feelings.

We also know we cannot truly "fight fire with fire" when it comes to dealing with other angry people. As tempting as it is to explode, meeting injustice with the cool, calm waters of love and compassion does far more than adding the heat of our anger to the situation.

How can we access love when what we feel is bitterness and resentment? How do we access love when we want to get even with someone for the pain they have caused us?

This is a supernatural process. I don't know if I can find love and compassion apart from God working in and on my heart. For me it requires letting go of the desire to get even and cause another person pain. It requires prayer and willingness to let go of whatever we believe this other person deserves for hurting us.

Don't get me wrong. I'm not saying you must lie down and let others trample on you. I am affirming the importance of caring for yourself—and your obligation to care for yourself.

I believe it is also imperative that you guard your heart at times. Scripture tells us: "Above all else, guard your heart, for everything you do flows from it" (Proverbs 4:23). Guarding my heart means I will watch what flows into it and what flows out of it. I want love and kindness to flow out of it, so am careful to associate only with those who bring love and kindness into my life.

What if you find yourself in severe relationship stress, where your mate does not tend to your heart? This situation calls for you to diligently guard your heart even more. You must fervently protect yourself, setting healthy boundaries. Again, if you will do this, positive change is possible.

The Path Forward

In this chapter you have learned that relationship stress is caused by and produces anger. Your anger must be transformed. You must take responsibility for your anger and explore the deeper, more vulnerable emotions hidden below the surface.

Each of us must take responsibility for our emotions and choose our perceptions and perspective. Consider again that you can have a profound impact not only on your mood and mind-set, but on your mate and family as well. Will you choose to be someone who embraces their feelings, affirms them, and then communicates them even if they don't receive a rousing welcome? Will you choose to be authentic in how you relate first and foremost to yourself and subsequently to others?

This is the only way.

Let's now continue our journey toward understanding the impact of being lost, alone, and searching for community.

EIGHT

LOST, ALONE, AND SEARCHING FOR COMMUNITY

*Loneliness is such an omnipotent and painful threat
to many persons that they have little conception
of the positive values of solitude and even at times
are very frightened at the prospect of being alone.*

—ROLLO MAY

I can think of only one thing worse than losing my health—losing my health while feeling abandoned, without the comfort, companionship, and community of others.

Relationship stress, as you've been discovering, wreaks havoc on your body and mind. This psychosomatic illness is debilitating in and of itself, but when endured alone it becomes all the more painful.

That's what this chapter is about: What it's like to be alone with relationship stress and the physical and emotional dis-ease that comes with it.

Loneliness is debilitating. We know this. Study upon study has illustrated the paramount importance of being emotionally connected to others. You must remember that it is possible to feel alone and still be surrounded by people. This loneliness is different from being alone with no one around.

The loneliness we will explore in this chapter is the fear that what you are experiencing—severe relationship stress and the toll it is taking on your body—can never be fully understood by others. Whether or not this is actually true, it feels true. You feel you can never fully share the truth of who you are with others.

This, then, is the greatest loneliness—the fear that you will never be fully known. The sense you have that you cannot fully reveal who you are to others for fear they would never understand. The sense that no one can fully understand your stress and trauma. You work amid many people, have family all around, and you may even be in a life-long marriage, and yet you still feel a deep, pervasive sense of loneliness.

This is profound loneliness.

Loneliness Defined

Loneliness is generally defined as a state of being alone and feeling sad about it. It occurs in all of us from time to time. We feel lonely when we move from one location to another or from one job to another, or perhaps when we lose a friendship or love relationship.

These experiences are different, however, than the loneliness that occurs from relationship stress and the physical problems occurring simultaneously. You may feel this pervasive sense of loneliness as a result of your longstanding relationship stress; and ironically, this long-standing loneliness may also be largely responsible for your physical problems, which then add to your sense of loneliness.

Loneliness becomes a circular problem; the more we feel alone, the more acutely we feel our physical pain. The more we feel our physical pain, the more alone we feel.

Our pain is further amplified by the deep need we all have to connect. It isn't just connecting that we're after, though. We have an innate desire to connect in a meaningful way. We want people to "get us." We want to be understood and get feedback that what we are experiencing is understandable, even normal. When others don't get us, we feel alone.

Recently I was riding with my wife from Seattle to our home on Bainbridge Island. Emotionally triggered by something, I remembered a painful memory from years ago, something I thought I had long since dealt with and forgotten.

Caught up in my momentary and surprising emotional distress, I began to cry, and my wife, Christie, noticed and asked me what was wrong. I became anxious, wondering if she would accept me. My emotional reaction, untethered to any specific event in the here and now, was very real; but I wasn't able to articulate exactly why I was having that reaction.

Christie handled the situation perfectly. She listened, asked gentle questions, and helped me process this grief from my past. She helped me make sense of my reaction and forged a strong bond with me.

Gretchen Rubin, in her article "7 Types of Loneliness (and Why It Matters)," says, "To be happy, we need intimate bonds; we need to be able to confide, we need to feel like we belong, we need to be able to get and give support."[1]

Christie created the perfect healing container for me. Look closely at what she did for me:

1. *She showed her concern for my welfare.* She noticed me crying and wanted to know what was troubling me. She showed that she cared about me.

2. *She gently asked questions.* In gently asking questions she created safety for me to explore my feelings on a deeper level. Asking *why* can be a very revealing experience.

3. *She validated my experience as normal.* When I shared about the troubling experience, and how I had been wounded by it, she showed compassion and concern. She let me know that anyone would be troubled by such an experience and that my response was normal.

4. *She guided me into an additional step for healing.* She offered that I might now choose to see the experience differently, nudging me forward in my life. I no longer needed to carry shame and blame, but rather loving-kindness for myself.

What Christie did for me in those initially difficult ten minutes was healing and powerful. She demonstrated the healing power of validation.

The Power of Validation

Few of us think about the power of validation, but we know when we've received it and when we haven't.

We have all had, at one time or another, the feeling of being validated—where we feel accepted, honored, and empowered. We know the exhilaration we feel when we share a thought and another affirms our thoughts. While they may or may not agree with us, they "get us."

Feeling validated connects us to others. Feeling validated for our thoughts, feelings, and experiences creates a feeling of oneness with others. We feel cared for and connected; and in turn we care for and connect with others.

Dr. Shefali Tsabary, in her article "The Power of Validation," says, "There is nothing that creates a greater inner schism than an emotion that is dismissed, or worse still, denigrated, and invalidated...We have all encountered situations where someone says something to us or does something to us that completely nullifies our sense of self. For that one moment, their power to reduce us to a sense of nothing is absolute. Their words like a sword pierce into our core, slashing away at any sense of worth, integrity or dignity."[2]

As much as we might think we are validating another, often we are not. While we may think we are listening well and we quickly respond to the other with, "I understand," most often we are neither listening nor understanding. More often than not, we try to connect with one another in fragmented moments rather than soft, supportive times. We forget that it is really up to the other person to say, "Yes, you get me," not us trying to convince them that we understand them. The difference is subtle, but important.

Stages of Validation

Much work has been done to advance the idea of validation, including research from Marsha Linehan, who is known for her pioneering work in dialectical behavior therapy. Many others have also discovered that we are extremely poor communicators, especially when it comes to validation—a critical aspect in relational communication.

Linehan has written extensively on the issue of validation. Each stage connects us powerfully to another, and the absence of validation is an extremely disconnecting component in our relationships.

Here are the stages of validation Linehan found to be powerful links between people, as aptly summarized by Dr. Karyn Hall.[3]

1. *Being present.* It is critical to acknowledge your internal experience and sit with it, rather than run away and avoid it. Sitting with intense emotion is not easy and can be very uncomfortable. Being present to another person with intense emotion in a nonjudgmental way is additionally very healing.

2. *Accurate reflection.* When communicating with another, summarize what you have heard from someone else or summarize your own feelings. When done in an authentic manner, with the intent of understanding the experience and not judging it, accurate reflection is validating. We might say, "I sense that you are feeling very confused with what to do next."

3. *Mind reading.* Here we guess what another person might be thinking or feeling. After listening intently to another, we offer a guess with compassion. We could say something like, "I'm guessing you might be feeling very sad about the news you've just gotten," thus validating them.

4. *Understanding the person's behavior in terms of their history and biology.* Our experiences and biology influence our emotional reactions. We reflect to the person we are validating that we have some understanding of their history and link their current reaction to their past. We might say "Given what's happened to you in the past, I can understand why you might be frightened to make this change in your life."

5. *Normalizing or recognizing emotional reactions anyone would have.* Here we normalize a person's reactions, confirming that "anyone would feel the same way." Since we all want to know that our reactions are understandable,

hearing about the normalcy of our reactions is very gratifying and validating. For example, a validator might say, "Anyone would be frightened about speaking in front of a large group of people."

6. *Radical genuineness.* Here we understand what someone is feeling on a very deep level. Perhaps you've had a similar experience and can share your understanding based on that similar experience. Perhaps you are touched by the power of their experience and show your compassion and validation by your presence and body language. You might say, "I had a similar experience when my mother died."

These stages of validation are powerful connectors to others. We are all desperate to feel connected, and even more for those experiencing feeling emotionally and physically unwell.

Emotional Invalidation

Imagine feeling alone, being physically and emotionally unwell, and desperately seeking validation. Imagine being in a relationship, or cluster of relationships, that are not only dissatisfying but are literally making you sick. Now add to this being met with invalidation when you seek validation.

Instead of a soft, warm, kind expression of acceptance, you receive a chilly and distant rebuff. The very act of being invalidated can, by itself, feel traumatizing.

You may believe these are strong words, even hyperbole. But these are real experiences. Emotional rebuff and rejection can be traumatic.

Again, it is critical to remember that we all *need* validation. We are hardwired for it. As infants we long for emotional attunement with our primary caregivers. As we grow we look into our parents' eyes for loving affirmation and support. Moving into adulthood, still longing to be heard, appreciated, and validated, we need to feel and believe that our perceptions are normal.

Sadly, many feel invalidated on a frequent basis. Many open up, seeking validation, only to experience rejection and simplistic platitudes.

Let's consider this list of some of the common ways we are invalidated, leaving us feeling even more alone and abandoned:

- *People assuming they know what we are thinking and feeling.* People don't take the time to ask what we are feeling or how an experience has impacted us. Someone might say, "I know how you feel about your mother."

- *People lying to us to protect us.* People tell us what they think we want to hear to avoid upsetting us. Of course, they are actually protecting themselves and hurting us in the process. Someone might say, "I really enjoy your family" when they do not.

- *People doing for us what we should do for ourselves.* Sometimes people will think for us, act for us, or make decisions for us, when we should be doing those things for ourselves. The husband says, "Karen can do that for you, no problem."

- *People attribute motives to us that are inaccurate and crazy-making.* People will tell us they know why we did something when this is not their right. This feels invasive and incredibly invalidating. Someone might say, "You made that decision because you were mad at your boss."

- *People judge our actions.* People criticize and judge our actions or feelings, ridiculing us or shaming us in the process. Someone might say, "That sure was a foolish decision."

- *People nonverbally invalidate us by rolling their eyes dismissively.* People will dismiss our truths by being impatient with us or nonverbally criticizing what we are saying and what is true for us.

These are just a few of the ways people invalidate our experience, leading to loneliness. If you are having these experiences, feeling emotionally and physically vulnerable, you will be even more prone to feeling isolated and misunderstood, adding to your lack of well-being.

Ostracized by Our Community

If gentle loving-kindness and validation are needed for healing and feeling connected—the antidote to loneliness—the opposite, feeling ostracized, pushed away by others, certainly damages our feelings of connection and acceptance.

If you're like me, even the notion of being ostracized is repulsive. Who would even consider ostracizing another human being? While this may not be a conscious process on the part of most people, we do ostracize—all of us.

We ostracize through the horrific power of racism, sexism, ageism, and the many other forms of judging others for their differentness. Bigotry is sadly still alive and flourishing and is very painful to the recipient.

Have you ever ostracized another person? As I reflected on the possibility that I push away from those emotionally or physically less stable than I consider myself, I thought of a common occurrence.

Consider your reaction to going to the hospital. If you're like me, you avoid going to hospitals. The sights and sounds of the sick make me feel uncomfortable. I much prefer to be around people who are vibrant, alive, and well.

How about nursing homes? Same thing. I don't generally like the sights and sounds of the elderly and infirm. Again, I much prefer to be around those who are physically alive and vibrant.

Perhaps you avoid those who are different from you by virtue of their race, religion, or socioeconomic status. Whatever the difference, you may push away from them and feel more comfortable in a homogeneous group.

Let's look at an example that many of you may be able to relate to. If you have experienced chronic relationship stress and carry the physical and emotional consequences of that, you feel less well than many others. You notice the difference. Acutely aware of your pain, you know you lack a certain vitality. You are painfully aware of being treated differently than others.

Subsequently, perhaps you avoid people because of these emotional and physical challenges. Let's bring our focus back to those experiencing severe relationship stress and its physiological impact. Do you think they feel "different" than others? I assure you, they do.

Many, being part of a community such as a church or extended family, have a sense of being part of that community and yet do not feel supported or understood by that community. They feel like they are on the outside looking in, not fully understood or accepted.

Susan

Susan was at one time a vivacious, outgoing woman. The middle child with an older brother and younger sister, she enjoyed both school and her extracurricular activities.

Susan's life was not perfect, however. In fact, while she was growing up, her home life was chaotic because her father struggled with alcoholism. This led to intense conflict between her parents. She became an extrovert as a way of coping. She became socially active in order to avoid the conflict happening in their home.

"I did anything I could to be away from home," she said. "It was crazy and unsafe at home, so I joined every possible club or activity. I hated being at home."

"How do you think that has affected you today?" I asked.

"I still run from conflict," she said. "When my husband is upset, I run. When the kids stress me out, I run. I don't like stress, and now I'm stressed out from all of my avoidance. My husband is unhappy, and I can see why. I don't know that I would want to be married to me."

"How are you doing physically?" I asked.

"I've always had a nervous stomach," she said. "I was anxious as a kid, and I'm anxious now. If I'm not careful I can drink too much as a way of coping with my anxiety. I've got to learn to talk about problems, and I've got a lot of them."

As we explored her history she reiterated that belonging came easy for her as she had a wide circle of friends and was part of numerous groups. This continued into her adult life, where she was active in college and then became active in church and civic groups. Maybe she was overactive.

But that was then; things are different now.

Susan started counseling as a young adult, when she began experiencing episodic anxiety and depression. Her struggles seemed to be situational depression and anxiety stemming from unresolved feelings about her father's alcoholism and parental conflict and subsequently regarding a husband who also abused alcohol. She developed a pattern of drinking during her most stressful times.

Susan had always coped with her significant issues by keeping busy—busy with her real estate career, busy with church involvement, and busy in civic groups. Now, at age 45, she is having more physical symptoms, and her doctors are having difficulty diagnosing and treating them.

"I'm not doing well," she shared with me. "I don't know exactly what's wrong, but I feel down more often than I used to. I'm more anxious than I ever remember being, and I'm not as happy. My kids have left the nest and that may be part of it. Menopause may be part of it. My husband's drinking may be part of it. I know I don't feel happy, and that makes me unhappy."

"Has anything else changed?" I asked.

"I'm not as involved as I used to be in activities," she said. "I've pulled out of a few commitments because I don't feel well. I don't feel accepted like I did before. I don't think people understand what I'm going through. How can they, since I don't understand it either?"

"Tell me more about what you're going through," I said.

"I just don't feel healthy," she said. "I hurt more and things get to me more than ever. People upset me. My husband makes me mad, and I wonder what's going to happen with our marriage. The people I work with annoy me more than before, and my body is starting to age. I hate that. Plus, I don't feel accepted or understood by anyone. No one really understands me, and I'm not sure I understand myself."

Reject Me, Reject You

Clearly Susan has never dealt effectively with her problems. She has either stuffed or acted out her feelings for years, and now they have begun catching up with her. Finally she's begun experiencing debilitating anxiety and depression, certain signs that something is wrong.

Whether it is real or imagined, Susan feels rejected by others. She feels misunderstood. Were people being more rejecting, or was she rejecting others?

I listened carefully as she continued.

"I don't really want to share my story when I don't feel understood," she said, "and I don't think anyone really understands me. It may all be in my head, but I'm really afraid people won't appreciate what I'm going through. It's complicated."

"But can't they understand your story if you share it with them?" I suggested. "I know a lot of people in very challenging relationships and it's affecting them terribly."

"I've found people don't really understand what it's like to be in both emotional and physical pain," Susan said. "So at some point I just began pushing away. Maybe I'm pushing them away before they push me away. Maybe I'm really afraid of getting close. I don't know."

Can you see the circular problem? Susan feels rejected and subsequently rejects others. The more she rejects others the more they reject her. The pattern continues and escalates, leaving her feeling more and more isolated, lonely, and lost.

Dr. Henry Cloud addresses this phenomenon in his book *Changes That Heal.* He writes about the issue of emotional attachment, noting that those who are emotionally detached live in a state of perpetual hunger, leading to them protesting.

> The pain that lonely, isolated people feel is a good thing, for it points to a vital need...If isolation continues too long without relief, the protesting person moves into the second stage of depression and despair...If depression and despair continue long enough without anyone intervening to relieve the loneliness, the third stage of detachment sets in. People who reach this stage are detached both from their own need for others and from the outside world. They are out of touch with themselves at a very rudimentary level; at times they no longer feel alive.[4]

This helps explain why someone might push away from others.

Feeling misunderstood and rejected, they become angry. Their anger, combined with distorted thinking in the form of "bad moods," repels them further from others, and from any possible source of nourishment and acceptance.

Seeking Acceptance

We are all desperate for acceptance and validation.

I crave acceptance and make no bones about it. The most pertinent ways I seek acceptance currently are through my efforts to be a good husband and a good writer.

Having experienced a failed marriage, I want to do much better the second time around. The doubts of what I could have done differently, the failures I remember, and knowing there are failures outside my awareness haunt me at times.

Now, for many different reasons, I want to do better. In both arenas of husbanding and writing, my wife, Christie, is my judge. She is the one who will indicate whether I am doing my part to be a great husband; and, since she is my primary editor, she determines whether my writing meets her standards.

I am anxious about both roles. But we've adopted a trick that helps me greatly in my role as a writer, taken from Benjamin and Rosalind Zander's book *The Art of Possibility*.[5]

In their book, Benjamin Zander, conductor for the Boston Philharmonic Orchestra, shares how at the outset of his classes at New England Conservatory he assured his students they would all get As for the course. The only requirement, he shares, is that each student had to write a letter to him, post-dated, stating what they had learned and why they deserved the grade.

Zander found, as have I, that when the students knew they would get an A, they could relax and settle into real learning. Christie has applied the principle to her editing with some slight modifications. She has assured me that my latest chapter submitted will eventually "get an A" if I apply myself, perhaps repeatedly, to making it a worthy project. Knowing I am accepted and that my words—these precious, valued, chosen words—will receive acceptance helps me relax and settle into writing.

Zander acted on what we all know: We long for acceptance. We long to be understood, valued, and appreciated for who we are. We want our individuality to be prized and even cherished. If we are accepted and cherished, we show up. If not, we shrink back. Showing up is better.

Lonely in Church

You might think the church would be a place where we could all show up, brave and fearless. You might think the church, one of the primary gathering places for Christians, would be the safest place on earth for us to feel completely safe and accepted.

Sadly, this is often not the case.

Many churches tend to be places where people gather for worship and fellowship, which is good, but they are *not* places to be transparent. Many come dressed in their facades, acting as if they have it all together.

Tragically, church also tends to be a place of rejection and judgment. While this goes completely against principles of Scripture—which directs us to accept and love others—most don't really accept the challenge. Our behavior doesn't match our beliefs. While we may believe in the principle of loving everyone, we often do the opposite.

Most churchgoers admit this if we are being completely honest. We mutter about those who are different. We voice criticisms as we walk away from gatherings of people. Knowing how shallow some will be, we subsequently guard ourselves.

Chuck Swindoll was one of the first Christians to write about this duplicity in his 1984 book *Dropping Your Guard.*[6] He believes we have a mask for every occasion, and this still seems to be true. He writes about people being phony, mostly out of fear of being really known.

Pastor Matthew Sickling also believes people wear masks. He writes, "Perhaps someone you love is facing an illness or a situation that scares the living daylights out of you but you don't want anyone to know it. So when someone asks how you're doing you smile and say 'I've never been better' when in reality you've never felt worse." He goes on to quote the apostle Paul, who said, "That is why, for Christ's sake, I delight in weaknesses, in insults, in hardships, in persecutions, in difficulties. For when I am weak, then I am strong" (2 Corinthians 12:10).[7]

From a Physician: Dr. Tyson Hawkins, Internist

I don't think there is any doubt that humans are social beings. The degree to which they enjoy socializing may differ (introvert versus extrovert), but neither group enjoys loneliness. Loneliness refers to the difference between the amount of social contact and intimacy you have and the amount you want. And the data is pretty clear: Loneliness is not good for our health!

Loneliness and social isolation were linked to an increased risk of stroke and heart disease, according to a review of studies published in *Heart*. The data showed that loneliness, social isolation, or both were associated with a 29 percent increased risk of heart attack and 32 percent greater risk of stroke. The risk was similar to that of light smoking or obesity, according to the researchers.[8]

A meta-analysis published in 2015 showed adults who have few social contacts (who are socially isolated) or feel unhappy about their social relationships (who are lonely) are at increased risk of premature mortality. Studies estimated this increased risk at about 30 percent on average.[9]

Glenda is a 78-year-old woman who came to see me recently. She had been suffering with a cough for the past four weeks and was getting pretty fed up. She had been evaluated by several other providers and was not happy with the answers she was receiving. In addition to the cough she also expressed concern regarding fatigue and insomnia. I had not seen Glenda in several years and was unfamiliar with her current life circumstances.

She divulged that she was now living independently because her husband had recently been admitted to a memory care unit due to advancing dementia. She had been his full-time caregiver for the past several years as his memory failed. I asked her if she had children or other family in the area, and she said no. She was now alone. And, quite honestly, she had been alone for several years because her husband was not really "all there."

She told me she had tried to reach out to neighbors in recent years but did not feel reciprocation. She had not made any friends over the years. She was disappointed in her neighbors for not taking a more active role in her life. She had even gone so far as to bake sweets and share them with neighbors as a show of goodwill, to no avail. She was becoming increasingly discouraged.

She was now suffering the consequences of loneliness. She was anxious and had a difficult time sleeping. She felt exhausted most of the time. She was losing weight. She was a shadow of the strong, resilient, energetic, and amiable woman she had once been. And she was scared. She was certain there had to be something wrong with her and was looking for answers. This cough was just the latest manifestation, and it was to her the harbinger that something worse was going to be discovered.

Loneliness can have severe consequences. We are not meant to live alone. Too much time "in our own head" in self-reflection can lead to excessive stress and worry. We use other people, intentionally or not, as sounding boards and gauges for our symptoms, which can be a healthy dynamic. I can't tell you how many times I have seen somebody in clinic after their loved ones urged them to come in due to progressive symptoms they had been ignoring or explaining away as "normal aging." Sometimes it is, and sometimes it is not. We could all use some form of barometer to help us understand normal aging and what to expect.

Fortunately Glenda's cough turned out to be nothing more than a postviral postnasal drip that cleared up with some saline irrigation. The bigger issue, however, was her social isolation and the impact it was having on her health. We spent the majority of our next visit strategizing ways to increase her social network.

We are not meant to be alone. The medical literature is clear—the socially isolated suffer an increased risk of death, heart disease, and stroke. Lonely people also sleep poorly, experience severe depression and anxiety, have reduced immune and cardiovascular functioning, and exhibit signs of early cognitive decline that grow more severe over time. Reducing social isolation and loneliness can have a profound impact on a patient's physical and mental well-being.

The Healing Power of Community

We all know the answer to loneliness. We must connect, even when doing so means being humble, open, and transparent. This requires trust.

Susan needs to open up and find support and care from those in her community. She must do what we all must do—reach out and allow others to care for us just as we care for them. Her first step was seeking counseling, and now she is on her way to becoming more connected and less lonely.

The powerful book *Band of Brothers* by Stephen Ambrose speaks dramatically about the impact of community. While the book is set during World War II, it chronicles the lives of the men of Easy Company who fought behind enemy lines in France on D-Day, knocking out cannons on Utah Beach and ultimately capturing Hitler's headquarters at the Eagle's Nest in Berchtesgaden.

The story shares how these men hated the blood and carnage of war but fought mightily not to let each other down. They suffered together, sacrificed together, and prayed together. Ultimately, they won together.

We intuitively know that our suffering and loneliness is halved when shared with another. We feel a great measure of relief when someone calls asking how we are, caring enough to listen patiently for our answer. When they don't hurry us, when they go beyond our first answer and ask a second question, we may be surprised but settle in to share the depths of our being. We are, in some measure, healed by a listening and attentive ear.

Those living with physical and emotional distress experience even greater distress from being alone with their suffering. Your suffering can be mitigated as you reach out and find those who might care for you. While you may initially tell yourself, *They are too busy to care,* be careful, for everyone is in a similar spot. We are all hardwired to be connected and long for friendship. Assume there is someone, perhaps many someones, waiting to be discovered and anxious for friendship.

The Path Forward

Relationship stress is aggravated by loneliness. We were not created to be alone. From the early church to the present day, we are all individuals longing to be part of a larger community. We long to belong.

Consider the ways you validate and invalidate others. Reflect on what you might do to increase your sense of community. Look around at the many opportunities in your world. Do you live in a neighborhood with opportunities to create friendships? Are you involved in a church with many groups gathering for different purposes? Are you ready to learn something new, like a foreign language, a musical skill, or cooking expertise?

People are gathering—that's what we do. You can view most groups as exclusive or as opportunities to be involved. Reach out, making an opportunity. There's a chance you will not be invited in, but a stronger chance you will.

Let's now continue our journey toward healing your relationships, mind, and body.

Nine

HEALING RELATIONSHIPS, MIND, AND BODY

Healing yourself is connected with healing others.

—YOKO ONO

L ife is difficult. Many of us have let out a sigh of understanding and validation to those words. Life is, indeed, difficult.

I would follow them with, "Relationships are difficult." Anyone who has been in a significant relationship can certainly attest to the truth of those words as well. And we are all in relationships (unless we've chosen to live as a hermit in the backwoods of Alaska).

Yet, as much as we might utter cross words about the challenges of relationships, as often as we stomp our feet in exasperation, most of us find ourselves in search of connection. We search for love, gravitate toward friendships, and long to be fully accepted by others.

Most want to belong, to be part of a community. We tend to live in neighborhoods, participate in social functions, marry, and seek good friends.

Not only do we believe somewhere deep in our soul that we want to love and be loved, but we also believe these relationships have something to offer us that we cannot find anywhere else.

This chapter is about relationships—the kind that offer solace and comfort and the kind that bring tension. We will explore what makes a healthy relationship and the indications that a relationship is either going bad or going to go bad.

The chapter is about how relationships can heal or hurt, build us up or tear us down. They can be a place of solace and protection, or they can leave us wildly unprotected and vulnerable to the pressures of life. Ultimately relationships can be a refuge from the challenges of life and the primary places we heal our wounds.

A Search for Completion

You may wonder if I am setting expectations too high for relationships. Perhaps. You will determine that for yourself.

Relationships come in all sizes and shapes. Most of us will experience marriage at some time in life. Most of us will also experience family, friendships, or work relationships.

Each venue gives you the opportunity to learn something about yourself. Why do you choose the friends you do? Why do you choose to move close to your family or far away? Why do you gain pleasure out of close attachment, or renewed energy from time spent alone?

In all these situations, like many people, you may be on a search for completion. Most of us recognize aspects of our character that need strengthening. We realize we're not as tolerant as we should be, or perhaps recognize we need a boost in self-confidence. We tend to gravitate toward others who offer something to us, something that might complement us in some way.

On the topic of marriage, I'm reminded of the words of Alain de Botton in his novel *The Course of Love*: "Love means admiration for qualities in the lover that promise to correct our weaknesses and imbalances; love is a search for completion."[1]

Is it possible, with all the theories that abound about how we select our marital partners, that we are on a search for completion? His words certainly resonate with me. Is it possible that in the choices we make in friendships we are also on a quest for completion? I think so.

Entering marriage again after a season of being single, I was much more "mature." I knew more about what I was looking for in a mate. With the help of years of experiences, wins, and losses, I believe I had a larger perspective to draw from as I sought love.

It has been more than 15 years since I met Christie and fell in love. I dated her for some time before broaching the M-word and making a lifetime commitment. I wanted to be sure. Nonetheless, I became sure, not in part because of de Botton's notion that love completes us.

Using de Botton's theory on love, I'll briefly share my own affirmation for his position:

- She was an extrovert, in contrast to my introversion.
- She was centered and stable, in contrast to my restless nature.
- She was open and exploratory spiritually, in contrast to my narrow perspective.
- She navigated safely and trusting through the world, in contrast to my conservative fearfulness.
- She lived boldly, in contrast to my reserved nature.
- She let go, in contrast to my holding on.
- She trusted and believed, in contrast to my questioning.

Please notice that I make no judgments about either of our natures. Christie is who she is and I am who I am. But we do, most often, complement one another nicely.

Relationships by Design

Relationships not only offer us a unique lens with which to view ourselves, but they also offer us some kind of complement. They can stretch us into becoming more than we are, a blueprint to building ourselves into the people we were created to be.

They can challenge us to see the world through a different lens, offering us opportunities to grow. Is it possible that God places people in our path in order to challenge us in some way? Is it possible that relationships, of all sorts and sizes, are part of God's creation? That every encounter is a chance to "go to school," learning what we might and even must?

Recently I made a new acquaintance. His name is Lee. He is 20 years younger than I am and not someone I would have befriended years ago. Today this new friendship feels right.

My wife, Christie, and I live in Mexico during much of the winter.

This year, while perusing the local e-zine about new things to do in Sayulita, I found an advertisement for a chocolate-making class. I mentioned the class to Christie and asked if she would be interested—she readily agreed, always eager to participate in some artistic endeavor. We signed up for the class and were excited to attend.

I was certain the chocolatier was a woman, and I even misremembered "her" name as Gina, or something like that. I had stereotyped pictures in my mind of what chocolatiers might look like, how they might live, and their personality.

Influenced undoubtedly by the movie *Chocolat,* I thought "she" might be 40, working in a large room filled with chocolate bars, truffles, and various other chocolate concoctions. The room or kitchen, perhaps entire neighborhood, would be filled with the glorious aroma of chocolate.

Walking up to "her" casita I was warmly greeted by Lee, a slender, soft-spoken man who appeared to be fortyish.

"Can you tell me where Gina is?" I asked. "She teaches classes on making chocolate."

"Well," he said slowly with a sheepish grin, "I teach classes, but my name is Lee."

It took me a few moments to get Gina out of my mind, but I was immediately drawn to Lee. We became fast friends.

Christie and I proceeded to spend the next several hours with Lee, learning how to make chocolate, from bean to bar. He shared his passion about chocolate, as well as his love for Mexico, business, doing therapy, and what he called "the transformation of chemical processes as well as human processes."

How could we not become fast friends?

Subsequently Christie and I have spent many hours with Lee. Not only is he an alchemist, able to transform cacao beans into chocolate, but alchemically helps people transform bad relationships into good ones as well.

Why am I so taken with Lee? Why him? Why now?

The short answer is, I don't know. The longer answer is that he has much to teach me about adapting to the pace of life in Mexico; he can also teach me much about loving and learning, listening to one-self and others.

The Stages of Relationship

Considering my notion that relationships offer us something, per-haps an opportunity for completion, I asked myself, *Why has Lee shown up now? What might he offer me, and what might I offer him?*

Since we are at the newfound-friend stage, there is still much I don't know and may never know. Mark Knapp, a communications scholar, has offered insights into how we connect (and why) and how we come apart (and why) in his book *Social Intercourse: From Greeting to Good-bye.* He says relationships go through the following stages:

1. *Initiating.* Knapp says this stage lasts only 15 seconds or less and is based largely on physical appearance. We put on our best self and try to make a favorable impression.

2. *Experimenting.* In this stage we share bits and pieces of ourselves with others and they do the same with us. Individuals engage in small talk to determine if they have any common interests.

3. *Intensifying.* In this stage two people continue to experiment to see whether they have mutual affection and attachment. Further self-disclosure is part of this stage of relating.

4. *Integrating.* Once mutual affection has been confirmed, you begin transitioning into the integration stage of the relationship. Each shares more of themselves with the other and they establish themselves as friends.

5. *Bonding.* Here two people share more information with one another, and the friendship becomes public. The connection between the two is solidified, perhaps by marriage or some other arrangement.

Just as a couple comes together through a process, Knapp also discovered stages in coming apart. This is surely true in relationships marked by significant stress.

1. *Differentiating.* Differentiating is a process of disengaging or uncoupling. During this stage, differences between the relationship partners are emphasized and what they thought were similarities begin to disintegrate. Instead of working together, partners begin to become more individualistic in their attitudes. Conflict is a common form of communication during this stage.

2. *Circumscribing.* Communication decreases during this stage of relating. Perhaps because of conflict, individuals become more guarded and share less information with the other.

3. *Stagnating.* Communication in this stage decreases further as each predicts how the other will respond. They experience "ruts" in the relationship because they "know" how the other will respond, or at least they believe they know and don't like it. If a relationship stays in this stage long it signals an ultimate demise of the friendship or relationship.

4. *Avoiding.* In this stage people will avoid the other, each pretending the other does not exist. They become separate from one another physically, mentally, emotionally, and spiritually. They disengage from each other and move toward termination of the relationship.

5. *Terminating.* No longer are they receiving benefits from the relationship, and therefore they move to terminate the relationship. This may be done by consensus or one partner ending the relationship. Communication is marked by distance and disintegration.[2]

When Relationships Hurt

Don't we all wish every relationship could "work" and remain exciting forever? We all love the initial high of a new relationship. But this doesn't last. It cannot last.

Some relationships lose the bubble very quickly. Others lose it over time. Some relationships are troubled nearly from the beginning and go through a rapid course of coming together and then coming apart.

Others, the ones described in this book, are not usually so sudden. In my time as a marriage counselor, I've found that the majority of people coming to me for help in their relationships have enjoyed the "coming together" phases of the relationship and greatly disliked the "coming apart" stages.

As Knapp pointed out, coming together and coming apart are predictable; and when something is predictable, it is preventable. We would all do well to examine more closely the *whys* behind what tears our relationships apart. What are the ingredients of a relationship likely to hurt a couple so badly they will push apart, no matter how much they care about one another? What can be done to more securely hold a relationship together, assuming that is our goal?

All relationships succeed or fail for many of the same reasons. The same problems that cause a work relationship to disintegrate are the ones that cause a marriage to dissolve. Whether we are talking about a friendship, work relationship, or marriage, many of the same factors that make us bad business partners or colleagues will be the factors that spell doom for an intimate relationship.

What creates the "glue" to hold two people together and what dissolves that glue? Five critical ingredients—certainly not meant to be the final word on the topic—are absolutely necessary to hold any partnership together.

- *Communication.* Communication is key to any relationship. Not just any kind of communication, but deep, honest, and transparent sharing. The glue that holds relationships together is kind, compassionate, and collaborative sharing. We realize, and hold in our minds, that this relationship is important and fragile. It cannot withstand abusive or harsh language or language intended to harm. It cannot withstand flippant gestures, even if there is no intent to harm.

- *Respect.* Any relationship moving beyond the initiating stage must be marked by respect. Respect is the idea
that someone holds you in high regard and you know
it. Because they hold you in high regard, the language
they use with you, and about you, will be positive. Even
when times are challenging and you have reasons for concern, those feelings will be shared in a respectful way. You
remain secure about the other's view of you.

- *Admiration.* Closely related to the concept of respect is
the idea of admiration. We all want to be with people we
know have some level of admiration for us. I'm not talking about the "You can do no wrong" or "You walk on
water" kind of admiration. Rather, it's a sense that you are
admired for your positive traits. People who admire and
respect one another are likely to be friends at the least, and
maybe much more.

- *Caring.* Not only must caring be part of the package of
healthy connection, but so must feeling cared about as
well. Caring and feeling cared for must both be present if
the relationship is to advance. We have a sense that this
other person has our back. They can be relied upon to care
for us should the need arise—and it will.

- *Boundaries.* Finally, any partnership is built upon clear and
agreed-upon expectations. Sometimes these are spelled
out, letter by letter, and other times parts of the agreement are simply understood. Most relationships are based
upon trust, and that trust comes from knowing the other
will keep you safe and protect you from harm. You often
set boundaries about faithfulness, ways you both will be
treated, and how the relationship will advance. Healthy
boundaries create healthy relationships.

These are the bare minimum of what is expected to make a relationship strong, glued together. Some would add trust to the list; others

might even add fun and adventure. What is important is that two people agree on what the relationship will look like, whether it will advance and stay together, or whether it lacks too many basic ingredients and must dissolve.

Think it over and decide.

Jeff and Candace

Communication, respect, admiration, caring, and boundaries were all central issues of concern in Jeff and Candace's relationship. They struggled in each area and, subsequently, their relationship was in serious trouble.

Jeff and Candace have been married for more than 20 years, and he works as general manager for her father's electrical supplies store. Candace made an appointment to see me after a series of difficult encounters with Jeff that left her wondering what to do.

While Jeff married into the business, he has been there many years and treats it as his own. He harbors growing resentment over the fact that he has never been able to buy into the business and must still answer to her father. Her father has never officially given him shares in the company, and Jeff feels acutely dismissed by this.

Jeff rarely lets a day go by that he doesn't make some snide comment about her parents. He doesn't feel supported by Candace, and she doesn't feel supported by him. Both harbor growing resentment.

According to her, he takes more than his allotted sick time, is often late for work, and is disrespectful to her and her father, both to their faces and behind their backs. He has gossiped about them to other employees but denies doing this when confronted.

Candace's father is not a strong leader. According to Candace, her father frets about confronting Jeff and feels Jeff's resentment. Their problems at work have seeped into their marriage.

"I'm really tired of all the problems this family business has caused," Candace told me. "Jeff resents me and my dad, and I think we should be grateful for all they have done for us. I think he is ungrateful."

"What have you done to clear the air with him?" I asked.

"Not much," she said. "Talking to him is like talking to a brick wall.

Talking only seems to make things worse, so I sweep things under the rug. My dad talks to me about these problems and complains about Jeff, but won't confront Jeff. I'm caught in the middle."

"You know you have to have some honest discussions with both of them," I said. "You know you need to sit down and call out the elephants in the room. There is so much taking place, with each person believing they are in the right."

"I believe my loyalty should be with my husband, but his angry attitudes bother me. All of this is making me crazy. It's affecting my health, my marriage, and my relationship to my family. My boundaries are terrible. I know Jeff and I need to talk and come to an agreement about all of this. Maybe it's time we didn't work for my parents. I don't know anymore. I know my sleep is affected and I worry about this stuff all the time."

"Tell me about your health," I said.

"I am always anxious about this situation. I'm not sleeping well," she said. "I used to think clearly, but now my mind moves slowly. I worry about my future, wondering if this is what I have to look forward to. Will relationships work out in my family? I lie awake at night worrying, and when I see Jeff fall asleep in two minutes, I get even more annoyed."

She paused.

"I'm losing weight and I'm always irritable. I'm always tired too. My doctors are looking into a possible autoimmune disorder of some kind. I'm just not in control of my life."

"How is your relationship with Jeff?" I asked.

Candace laughed nervously.

"I act like things are okay, but I think we both know they're not," she said. "We both know this is taking a toll on our marriage."

"What do you mean?" I asked.

"He challenges my decisions, scoffs at my parents and their leadership, and this really hurts me. You would never know it, though. I mostly bury my feelings."

"But your body is keeping score, right?" I asked.

"Wow, I think you're right."

Hurting People Hurt People

Our emotions are always working, impacting how we think, feel, and react to situations. While we may fly through life, our bodies, minds, and emotions feel and record the impact. Our bodies and minds keep score, and the score adds up. We cannot continually sweep things under the rug.

It is easier to see a problem from outside of a situation. Listening to Candace, I can quickly see her dilemma; she is being pulled in two different directions of loyalty. I can see how communication is convoluted, further aggravating the problem.

Candace is acutely feeling the strain of being caught in the middle of Jeff and her parents. She cannot continue to hear his snide remarks and also know that her father is upset as well. They have got to solve these problems, or she must determine a way to get out of the middle.

This is the simple, straightforward answer to her problem. As you and I both know, life is rarely this simple.

She relies on her parents for her and her husband's financial livelihood, not to mention the love and respect she has for them. She is grateful for the opportunities they have given her and her husband. Yet there is ongoing, unresolved conflict.

Nonetheless, Candace must face her own fears and weaknesses. She must have some hard conversations with Jeff, clarifying roles, expectations for the way the company runs, and how she expects him to interact with her parents. She must share her feelings with him.

Likewise, she must also be ready to hear him and validate concerns he undoubtedly carries inside. She must be a safe place for him to share his disappointment, feelings of disrespect, and fears.

Additionally, Candace must ready herself for a conversation with her father and perhaps her mother, collaborating with her husband about their best course of action. The air must be cleared.

Candace is experiencing a great deal of anxiety. While she may tell me this is all resulting from the present situation, this is rarely the case, for her or for any of us. Past issues, and ways we have dealt with them or not dealt with them, impact today. Her avoidance of issues is a pattern for her, influencing every area of her life.

Anxiety, contained and denied, affects our bodies, minds, emotions, and, yes, relationships. I can imagine her anxiety impacting her marriage, her relationship to her parents, and her own mental, emotional, physical, and spiritual health. As with a pebble thrown into a pond, the ripples extend a long way.

Candace hurts, and subsequently she hurts others in the process. Those around her feel her tension. She has become more aware of her irritability as both her husband and father make more frequent complaints. It's time she owns the horrific impact this stress is taking on her. She must make some difficult decisions.

From a Physician: Dr. Tyson Hawkins, Internist

Research consistently shows that happily married people have lower levels of coronary heart disease (the world's number one killer) than divorced, single, or separated people.[3]

We have historically attributed this to the therapeutic benefits of a healthy relationship and its concomitant effects—something that happens at the same time as another thing—on chronic stress. However, recent research by Dr. Timothy Smith and Dr. Brian Baucom at the University of Utah provides an alternate way of looking at the correlation. They suggest many of the qualities that make people good at relationships, such as personality, level of emotional adjustment, and the like, make them more likely to be healthy, to deal with stress better, and to sleep better. So it may not be marriage that makes people healthy, but rather character traits. In the same way, character traits that damage one's health may also keep these individuals from being married.

Smith goes on to say, "There's substantial literature that suggests that improving people's management of chronic diseases like coronary heart disease can be made better or worse by how things are going in that relationship."[4] The effect is much less about how one monster marital tiff is going to give someone a heart attack and more about how a consistent routine of negative interactions is likely to have a stressful effect on circulation. Additionally, patients engaged in healthy relationships are more likely to be compliant with medication and follow-up appointments than those in toxic relationships where the reminders are considered adversarial and "nagging."

Smith also addresses the role disruptive sleep may have, stating, "Sleep disorders and insomnia are strongly predictive of heart health."[5] People whose marriages are happy tend to sleep better than those who are in conflict with a spouse, or who are lonely and brooding at night. They don't fight as much, and when they come home from a stressful day at work, they can calm down and give their circulatory system a breather.

Cardiovascular disease is just one example. I believe the same can be said for any chronic disease requiring attention to healthy behavior modification, medication compliance, and follow-up appointments and testing. I see this every day in my practice.

Judy is a 56-year-old smoker with a history of high blood pressure and high cholesterol. She is married to a controlling husband. She wishes she could spend more time with her friends, but her husband does not want her to leave the house or socialize without him. She wishes she could be more physically active, but her husband has no desire to join her. He wants her home with him but does not show her much attention when she is there. Her husband's demands on her time have curtailed her ability to either visit with friends or get more exercise. She wants to quit smoking but feels excessively anxious whenever she tries. She has tried medications, patches, gums, and hypnosis without benefit. She is convinced she smokes to handle the stress caused by her unhealthy marriage. She does not believe in divorce. In addition, she has gained nearly 20 pounds over the past year due to inactivity and "stress eating."

I am concerned for her cardiovascular health. I can treat the measurables, her high blood pressure and cholesterol, but I cannot lower her stress. We have discussed medications and counseling, but I'm afraid these may be insufficient. She tells me her husband is aware of his tendencies and is working on them. I only hope she's right.

Relationship stress, whether within the structure of marriage or not, clearly has an adverse effect on people's health. It increases the risk of serious medical conditions such as heart disease, stroke, and diabetes, and has an adverse effect on quality of life. I don't claim to have an answer to treating this condition, but I hope this book serves to increase awareness that this problem exists. The first step in treating a condition is identifying there's a problem.

Healing Your Relationships

I am thankful that we all have the power, and often the ability, to heal our relationships. You may disagree with me on the last part of that statement. Do we really have the ability to heal our relationships?

Yes and no.

It is not as easy as it sounds. However, I suggest much can be done if we utilize the skill and power we do have to the fullest. What if the issue is not so much skill as pride? What if many of the problems in relationships have to do with communication, respect, admiration, caring, and healthy boundaries?

Remember what Jesus said about division within kingdoms and within households? "If a kingdom is divided against itself, that kingdom cannot stand. If a house is divided against itself, that house cannot stand" (Mark 3:24-25).

Every relationship that prospers holds these principles dear—we must support and care for one another. We must remember that the sum of the parts is greater than the whole.

Dr. Walter Jacobson says this about healing relationships:

> Truly loving, nurturing and sustainable relationships are not happening for a great many of us. The reasons for this have to do with our ego getting in the way, with our unwillingness to be more thoughtful, tolerant and considerate, with our unwillingness to rise above the battlefield, to release our anger and resentments from the past, to effectively communicate, to negotiate differences and to establish, maintain and respect boundaries.

> I say unwillingness because although it may be difficult to
> do these things, we choose not to. Loving, sustainable rela-
> tionships are not the result of accidents or luck—they are
> the result of healthy choices.[6]

Notice that Dr. Jacobson says healing relationships is about getting back to basics—being more thoughtful, tolerant, and considerate
and being willing to rise above any battle. We will never communicate effectively if we come from a place of intolerance, pride, and
demandingness.

To arrive at this mental, emotional, and spiritual place, however,
means letting go. It's not so much learning new techniques as it is letting go of the barriers we cling to because of our pride, which rein-
forces a belief that a problem is not really ours, but outside of us. No,
we must be candid with ourselves and ask what we must do to remedy our distress.

Is fear getting in the way of Candace resolving matters with Jeff?
At first you might not think so. You might see her as she is prone to see
herself: Victimized by Jeff's arrogant and pushy attitude. You might
see her as being caught in the middle between her husband and her
parents.

But look deeper. Candace believes she should not *have* to work this
out with Jeff. Candace believes Jeff is clearly in the wrong and she is in
the right. She holds on to anger and resentment rather than stepping
up and taking care of business.

The bottom line is that this is Candace's problem to fix. She is the
one carrying anxiety around in her body. She is the only one who can
fix her problem. The solution must begin with her.

I don't want to make this sound simple, for it most assuredly is not.
But she can do it. She must do it. She has the power and capability to
change the way she views the problem and can use this situation as a
growth opportunity, which it certainly is.

Healed People Heal People

Just as hurting people hurt people, fortunately, healed people heal people. Not literally, of course. But we do have an impact on others, both for bad and for good.

You have the power to have an impact on healing yourself and every relationship you are involved in. You have the power to change how you interact with others; and if you manage that, you will change your relationships for the better.

Picture a mobile. Every moving piece impacts every other moving piece. When one piece moves and changes, every other piece moves and changes. Such is the nature of a family or any other community. Each person impacts every other person, for good and for bad. Emotions are truly contagious.

The concept of a mobile helps us understand why a dysfunctional or toxic relationship can have such a detrimental impact on each individual. We touch one another. We impact one another. We send good, positive impressions or negative, hurtful impressions. Emotions and attitudes are contagious.

Imagine you are part of many mobiles. Perhaps you're in a marriage mobile, a family mobile, a church mobile, a work mobile, and a mobile of friends. In each area, you are not only impacted but you impact. You receive toxic messages or good, healthy messages, and you also give out messages.

What if you were to be a positive influence on everyone you came into contact with? What if you made a decision to be a healing influence on every person who came into your world? You would be sending positive messages and influences and would receive the same.

I've shared before how my wife, Christie, positively jangles every mobile in her world, from the supermarket cashier to the guests who come to stay in our cottage. She *never*—and that is a strong word—misses an opportunity to jiggle the mobile of someone who enters her world. They invariably leave with a smile.

As you consider your world filled with many mobiles, or relationships all touching one another, consider what you need for your own healing. Remember that every relationship—every single one—affects you. These relationships touch you profoundly. Is the net sum of those encounters a positive gain or a loss?

The Healing Power of Relationships

It's true—we are affected by our relationships, for good and for bad. The good news, great news actually, is that we can influence this powerful variable in our well-being.

This book has largely been about how our relationships have the power to make us sick, and that is true. But we should also talk about how our relationships have the potential to make us healthy.

Linda and Charlie Bloom, in their article "The Healing Power of Relationships," cite such experts as Dean Ornish, Andrew Weil, Daniel Goleman, Jon Kabat-Zinn, Larry Dossey, John Robbins, and the Dalai Lama as those who purport that the quality of our relationships affects our well-being just as much as genetics, diet, exercise, and other healthy factors. The Blooms add:

> Most of us have experienced the pleasures and joys of giving enough to know it feels good to contribute to the well-being of others, whether we show that love by an act of kindness, an encouraging word, a caring touch, an expression of appreciation, or any of the other countless ways we humans have of touching the heart of another. Now, thanks to some important and compelling findings compiled by many researchers and scholars, including some of the aforementioned individuals, there is hard evidence that it not only feels good to create caring relationships with others, but that such connections have a profound impact on the quality of our physical as well as emotional health.[7]

It's true. Being in loving, healthy relationships adds years to your life and life to your years. Being loved is perhaps the single most important factor contributing to your sense of well-being.

This may not be immediately available to you, and if that is the case, you have some planning to do. It's possibly past time for you to sit down and evaluate the quality of your relationships. Remember, your relationships can make you hurting and unhappy, or healthy and vibrant.

The Path Forward

We have talked about relationships, the good, the bad, and the ugly. We have explored what takes them up and what takes them down. Fortunately, there are reasons for progressions and regressions made in relationships, and that gives us a choice about the quality of the relationships we have. While it may seem that our relationships spontaneously move forward and backward, most of this is actually within our control. This, in turn, gives us some power concerning our physical, emotional, and spiritual well-being.

I hope you are using this chapter to reflect deeply on your relationships, taking responsibility for changing how you interact in each of them. Bear in mind, you cannot change anyone, but you can change yourself. And when you do, others change. That's exciting.

Let's now continue our journey toward healing your relationship with God.

TEN

DISAPPOINTMENT WITH GOD

*The soul can split the sky in two, and
let the face of God shine through.*

—EDNA ST. VINCENT MILLAY

I was raised in church.

Not literally, of course, but very nearly so. My parents had me and my four siblings at church every Sunday morning and evening as well as for midweek services. If there was a church event, we were there.

Subsequently, I was raised with about 15 sets of parents. Divorce was virtually unheard of, and many parents felt freedom to speak into my life. To say I felt loved and close to these many families is an understatement.

As if that were not enough faith to pour into us, we were also expected to attend church camps during the summer. Church and God were an integral part of my DNA.

There was no clear beginning or end to church life, God, or worship. God was to be revered and worshipped. That's just the way it was. I don't know whether I felt God's unique and distinct presence or if God was just part of the family. Like the air I breathed, it never occurred to me to question God's presence.

My Parents' Faith

My parents had a strong and abiding faith that deeply influenced me. Like osmosis, their faith was my faith. In addition to church attendance, family devotions, and prayer at meals, their faith was mine until sometime in my adolescence.

I remember being a reflective, angst-filled teenager. In addition to questioning my appearance, my social skills, friends, and girls (sex), I began to distinguish my faith from my parents' faith.

I began to doubt. I doubted a lot.

My pastor, Carleton Peterson, made himself available for my ceaseless questioning. He patiently entertained my questions about prayer, the Trinity, Christ's death and resurrection, and other perturbing issues. I visited with him hour after hour, questioning everything pertaining to Christianity.

Pastor Peterson never forced his beliefs on me. He created space for me to think, doubt, question, and slowly arrive at my own faith. My parents did a wonderful job of allowing me room to doubt, and Pastor Peterson helped me navigate these murky waters.

My father believed what he believed, having sorted out his theological doubts years earlier. My mother was a deeper thinker. She had a quiet, firm grip on her faith.

In a most poignant moment, nearing the end of her life, I remember asking her about her readiness for death.

With her most loving and tender smile, the kind a knowing mother bestows on a son, she softly quoted 2 Timothy 1:12: "I know whom I have believed, and I am persuaded that He is able to keep that which I've committed unto Him against that day."

Oh, that I could sit with her just once more, hold her frail hands, and hear her echo those reassuring words!

Soul-Searching

With all my parents' teaching, guiding, and directing, I arrived at the place we must all arrive: You cannot have your parents' faith. It just doesn't work that way. If one could adopt their parents' faith, I certainly could have and would have done it because it would have been much easier.

But faith, by its very nature, is personal.

There are seasons of life when we are more inclined to do our soul-searching, and for me adolescence was that time. Adolescence is typically a stage of life when we throw off all that has been handed down to us and begin searching for our individuality.

That is certainly what happened to me. Adolescence was my first major crisis of faith. Adolescence is a time of crisis—a time of soul-searching. Those reading this book will also recognize your current season of life, when your bodies and minds are wracked with stress, as another crisis and a soul-searching period.

At two crisis points in my life I wondered who God was, where He was, and what in the world He was doing.

The first was adolescence, where nothing of the Christian faith made sense to me. Praying to a God I could not see, touch, or feel? Nonsense. Three persons in One? Nonsense. Trusting in this God to lead and guide me through the tumultuous times of puberty? Nonsense.

But I navigated through this troubled time with the caring direction of a pastor who had the good sense to simply listen. I came to believe that there actually could be a God who designed the universe, that there could be a holy Trinity, and that prayer could actually connect me to this mystery.

My second major crisis came with my divorce in 2001. Rejected by my wife, my church, and others claiming to be "loving, caring Christians," I questioned the church more than I questioned God. What happened to the loving, embracing, caring community I had known as the church?

I navigated this treacherous path with my faith intact, albeit tarnished a little. I discovered others who felt rejected by formal religion. I was reminded that people will be people—some good, some not so good. I found love from others in many different places, and my faith in God and humanity was restored. I searched for, and found, other caring, embracing communities of faith.

Shelly

Shelly hasn't fared as well when it comes to restored faith, and I can hardly blame her.

Fifty years old and married her entire adult life to Earl, Shelly came for her session seeking help for her faltering marriage. She immediately shared her feelings.

"I don't really have much hope left for my marriage," she began. "I'm not even sure why I'm here."

"What's going on?" I asked.

"Earl is 'old school,'" she began, looking at a few notes she brought with her. "He's loved in our church and is there for every service. He helps in every way, from driving the kids' bus to mowing the lawn. He'll do anything for the pastor but does next to nothing for me."

"Please continue," I said.

"I don't know if we love each other anymore," she said. "We are dedicated to each other, because that's what Christians do. We're just sticking in there and staying married no matter how we feel inside. But I've got a few good years left and I'm not at all sure I want to spend them with him. I've begun wondering if life would be better alone or with someone else."

"Why isn't Earl with you for this appointment?" I asked.

Shelly laughed.

"He would never go to counseling," she said. "He says that all our problems can be solved with prayer. If it can't be solved with prayer, he says, it isn't really a problem and I should just get over it."

"My goodness," I exclaimed. "That is hard to argue against."

"You're telling me," she said. "I can't argue with him. He's got a scripture for every problem and can talk his way out of anything. He won't accept criticism and turns every problem back on me. His bottom line is that I should pray more and be a better Christian. Furthermore, if I were a good Christian, he says, I'd be content and never upset him."

She paused, cleared her throat, and continued.

"He makes a pretty good case for himself, pointing the blame at me for all our problems. He quotes Scripture on being content in all our circumstances, and that one really guilt-induces me. Then he even threatens to have our pastor talk to me, as if I'm being a nagging wife by wanting more communication and emotional connection. I want him to take responsibility for the harsh ways he treats me, but that isn't going to happen."

"Sounds like his guilt-tripping works," I said.

"Oh, it works all right, and he works it," she said resentfully. "He knows what he's doing, and I resent him even more for doing it. But right along with my resentment comes my guilt. Along with my guilt come my headaches and heartaches. I'm more anxious than I've ever been and more and more unhappy."

Shelly is one of many women who are caught in the throes of distorted Christianity. Her husband uses Scripture to manipulate her. He believes in the scriptures he's quoting and in the direction he wants his wife to take.

Faith Healing

Shelly is in a very complex and challenging situation. Her husband's words are confusing to her: Part prophetic, part inspirational, part true, and part false.

"We *are* to be content in all circumstances," Shelly told me. "That's a true scripture. But does that mean I have to accept the way Earl preaches at me but doesn't really live out what it means to love me well?"

She paused again.

"He is always challenging me to be happy and that the Lord doesn't want me to be in emotional and physical pain. He actually believes physical pain may be punishment from the Lord for my attitude. Is he right?"

"No, Shelly," I said. "He is distorting Scripture. He's taking some truths and mixing them with his own theology and perspective."

"I don't know what to do with the scripture that says, 'We know that God causes everything to work together for the good of those who love God and are called according to his purpose for them'" (Romans 8:28 NLT).

"Could it be that God does work everything for our good, but that doesn't mean He *makes* all things happen the way they do?" I said. "We have free will. Certainly Earl is acting in ways that are contrary to many scriptures."

Shelly is trying valiantly to unravel a most difficult puzzle. Earl is like many men, using their positions and gender to overpower their mates. He uses his knowledge of Scripture to manipulate her. Like many women, Shelly is vulnerable and trying to make sense of it all. Meanwhile, she suffers emotionally and physically.

Out of Context

Earl may be a very good man, but he is taking Scripture out of context and using it to manipulate, and that is emotionally abusive. Not only is it emotional abuse, but it is also spiritual abuse.

It is no wonder Shelly is confused and suffering spiritually, emotionally, and physically. She is working far harder than she should to make sense out of her world. Rather than being a place of refuge, her faith has now added an additional component of confusion to her already confusing world.

To make matters worse, Shelly must ferret out the truth of Scripture from the twists and turns her husband uses to make Scripture say what he wants it to say. This is largely what makes it spiritual and emotional abuse.

Talking about emotional abuse in the Christian community, Elisabeth Corcoran writes in her article "Emotional Abuse in Marriage" that Christians often look at emotional abuse as different from physical violence. She notes that many mates, as well as friends in church, tell the emotionally abused woman to suck it up and pray more. She notes that any attempt to induce fear, guilt, or shame in a mate is emotionally abusive and should not be tolerated.[1]

Fighting against the harsh words of an abusive husband is one thing, but wrestling with God makes matters even more complicated.

"How do I know if my husband is messing with my mind?" Shelly added. "All his words make sense on some level. The result is always me feeling worse."

"That is the biggest clue," I said. "His words should edify you, Shelly, not tear you down. His words should bring encouragement and clarity, not discouragement and confusion."

"That makes sense to me," she said. "Still, it's hard to fight against God."

"You don't have to fight against God," I said. "Seek the truth in everything, and you will know what to do."

Thankfully, Shelly is a strong woman and she knows there is something amiss in what her husband is saying to her. While she has yet to determine what exactly is right, she knows what he is doing is wrong.

Toxic Faith

Shelly's faith, through no fault of her own, added a layer of problems for her. Her faith, again through no fault of her own, has become toxic. What had been a source of life and health for her was now tainted—her husband had brought something unhealthy into something pure and good.

Why do I say her faith has become toxic? Because she now is confused about her faith, believing she should never doubt God's love for her and believing if she were a better Christian she would have immediate peace and answers to all her prayers.

Stephen Arterburn writes about the beliefs of those who use God for profit, power, pleasure, or prestige—qualities of Shelly's husband!

Arterburn might say both Shelly and her husband, Earl, have symptoms of toxic faith. He describes the following symptoms of toxic faith:

- *Conditional love.* Believing God's love and favor depend on one's own behavior. This leads to a faith in one's self rather than a faith in God.

- *Instant peace.* Believing one should have instant peace regardless of one's circumstances. While our faith certainly offers us a "peace that passes understanding," we are also human and experience all the emotions that come with our various challenges.

- *Guaranteed healing.* Believing that our faith should bring healing. One's faith doesn't dictate that God must heal anyone. We cannot control God with our prayers.

- *Spiteful god.* Believing our problems are the result of some particular sin. All problems, of course, are not a result of sin. Pain is often a result of sin but not a punishment for something we've done or not done. Problems result from poor decisions as well as living in a broken world.

- *Irrational submission.* Believing we must always submit to authority. This has been particularly thorny for Shelly, who believes she should not only submit to her abusive husband but also to pastors who covertly and at times overtly support his power.

- *Passivity.* Believing that true faith means waiting for God to help and doing nothing until He does. This belief leads many to wait and wait rather than taking responsibility for making changes in their life.

- *Pollyanna perspective.* Believing everything that happens must be for our good. We must come to see that God allows bad things to happen, but not all that happens is necessarily good for us.

- *Vindictive god.* Believing God "hates sinners, is angry with me, and wants to punish me." While God may allow dire consequences to occur, He is not vindictive.[2]

As you can see, Shelly needs to sort out truth from lies, helpful information from distortions. She will likely need expert help in determining truth from fiction.

Healing from Spiritual Abuse

Shelly has some work to do, discerning the truths of what God has to say to her from the false notions concocted by her husband. Her journey is one many women are forced to take.

Sadly, no one can really recover from spiritual and emotional abuse until the abuse stops. I know these are hard words and may cause you to feel even more uncomfortable than you already do.

What are you supposed to do if you suspect spiritual abuse is part of your disappointment with God? Here are a few steps to take:

1. *Remove yourself, at least partially, from the abuse.* Many stay in abusive situations for a variety of reasons. You may doubt yourself and accept the abuser's words as truth. Step back, at a minimum, and begin to question what they are telling you.

2. *Get support.* Find a listening ear from someone you fully trust. You will know if they are speaking truth to you or adding to your confusion. Find someone with a solid faith who can help you sort out truth from fiction.

3. *Get perspective.* If you've been in an abusive situation for some time, it is likely that your perspective has become skewed and distorted. Again, read about spiritual abuse, talk to trusted friends, and get professional help to regain perspective.

4. *Establish healthy boundaries.* Tell your mate you no longer want him to speak into your spiritual life. While he will likely see this as rebellion and resistance, stand firm. Your spiritual life is your spiritual life. Own it and protect it.

5. *Establish your own spiritual journey.* Your faith walk is intimately personal. No two people have the same beliefs or journeys. Establish your own unique journey and cherish it. Ask God to reveal Himself in new and fresh ways to you.

Shelly will gradually find her own spiritual, emotional, and physical voice, but not without challenges. She will have to push against her husband and experience discomfort while doing it. Yet she has established a new path and has slowly begun to gain relief from the effects of abuse.

The Stages of Spiritual Faith

Shelly's spiritual journey was marked by the stages others have traversed as they sought out a new relationship with God. Just as there are stages in emotional and physical growth, many discover there are stages in their faith walk as well.

In his article "5 Stages of Spiritual Awakening," Dave Ferguson found that when people come to faith they pass through a similar set of experiences:

1. *Awakening to longing.* In this stage we reflect on the universal feeling that there's got to be more to life. Most feel a deep longing for love, purpose, and meaning. Any crisis in life, and yours certainly qualifies, can ignite this awakening again.

2. *Awakening to regret.* Here we experience our regrets, misgivings, and choices we wish we had never made. We review our lives and note the places and circumstances where we fall short of our ideals. Some get stuck for significant periods of time feeling sorry and sad about their lives.

3. *Awakening to help.* After trying to fulfill ourselves without God and ending up with regret over and over, we finally acknowledge something has to change. We come to the end of ourselves, hit bottom, and recognize our need for help.

4. *Awakening to love.* We discover that God loves us in spite of poor choices or disappointments. We may still experience a shadow of shame, doubt, and guilt as we struggle to believe we are loved and accepted just as we are.

5. *Awakening to life.* In this stage we realize through Jesus we can have life and life in abundance. Not only is our biological life full, but our spiritual life is full as well.[3]

As with most stages of life, we may navigate back and forth, making progress, lapsing back, and then moving forward again. Remember, any crisis can disrupt our current stage of life or of faith.

It is also important to note that the stages listed above are meant to give direction to our spiritual walk, not to indicate anything we must change. The stages can help us see where we are and what our next spiritual step might be.

Doubting Christians

Notice that the stages of spiritual awakening show movement—from longing to fulfillment, from regret to forgiveness, and ultimately from emptiness to abundance.

Nowhere do I see that we have to completely give up doubt or disappointment. Shelly still has doubts, though she believes God will see her through her crises. I certainly still have doubts on a rather regular basis.

One of my favorite religious authors, Kathleen Norris, has some thoughts on doubt and sacred ambiguity. In her book *Amazing Grace,* she tells how she shared many doubts with monks, but was surprised to find they were actually unconcerned with her weighty doubts and intellectual frustrations over Christianity.

> I had thought that my doubts were spectacular obstacles to my faith and was confused but intrigued when an old monk blithely stated that doubt is merely the seed of faith, a sign that faith is alive and ready to grow.[4]

This seems so true. These are words I shared with Shelly as she tried to make sense out of her disappointment with God and doubts that He would be enough for her. Did she have to redefine how she viewed God? Most definitely. Have I had to rethink how I view church and Christians? Absolutely. Have these questions been the seeds of new growth? Oh, yes.

From a Physician: Dr. Joshua Hawkins, Surgeon

"Oh, Doctor. I can't tell you how much we praise God for you. We have been praying that He would provide someone who loves Jesus to take care of Mom."

Wow. Pressure's on. Or is it?

I get these kinds of comments regularly from people who know Christ, who are dealing with tough illnesses. These moments are the fuel that keeps the fire going. I am extremely grateful I get to experience bodily healing through His boundless grace. I am so small, so limited, and yet He has chosen to use me in this way.

Surgery requires a relationship of profound trust. When I am privileged to care for one of His sheep, building that relationship is easy. We instantly connect on the deepest level built on shared values and worldview, based on belief in our loving Creator, who knows the number of hairs on our heads, and knows the hurts in our hearts and bodies. We also share the greatest hope that cannot be diminished; we know that whatever happens on this earth, we will one day join our Savior with new bodies without disease, in perfect union with Him, but also with each other in restored relationships.

I once had a limited understanding of what it meant to live out a life of evangelism, and I thought the only way to bring God glory was to work in ministry. I never wanted to be a surgeon. While I always wanted to be a physician, once I started living my life for Christ, I felt called in other directions. Many people long for a clear "calling" from God, for direction in life. I can attest to the fact that God's calling can be difficult.

Surgery is hard. I work very long hours and sacrifice endlessly for my profession. I even sacrifice my own health. I experience suffering daily, and death regularly. People put their faith in me, but I am fallible. Tim Keller, pastor of Redeemer Presbyterian Church in New York, put it this way: "Suffering dispels the illusion that we have the strength and competence to rule our own lives." I am reminded of that concept daily. God works in spite of me because of His great love for us.

Victor Hugo captures the immensity of God's love for us in *Les Miserables*, saying, "The supreme happiness of life is the conviction that we are loved; loved for ourselves, or rather, loved in spite of ourselves."[5]

I work as a surgeon in a small community. That means I don't get to separate work and life. I get to operate on my coworkers, my friends, my kids' friends' parents, the mayor of town, the hospital board members' spouses.

Sarah was one of my medical assistants. She came to work for me after I had cared for her as a patient. She'd had leukemia at age 22, and she needed a central line for chemotherapy and stem cell transplant. Through that short episode of care, we came to experience a glimpse into the mutual faith that directed our lives. When her cancer was in remission, she trained as an MA and came to work for me. Working with her was a joy. She was a light in a dark place. Patients loved her—her warm smile, her ability to make them laugh, and her genuine concern for their well-being. Our partnership was going well.

And then, unexpectedly, I became her surgeon again. She developed strange abdominal pains and was suddenly hospitalized. Recurrence of her leukemia was always in the back of our minds, but there was no easy way to make a diagnosis. A CT scan showed some vague changes in the omental fat in her abdomen. Worried and with nothing else to offer, I performed a laparoscopy and a biopsy of her abdominal fatty tissue. The results showed sheets of leukemia cells. Her cancer was back with a vengeance. I cried with her and her family. She died soon after at the age of 25. But between those tough first few days after her terrible diagnosis and the end of her life, she was an example of joy in suffering. She was one of the most selfless people I've ever known.

I would come to see her in the hospital, where she was clearly exhausted and in extreme pain, but she would barely allow me to ask about her. She always wanted to make sure I was getting by okay in her absence, and she asked with genuine concern about patients we had been caring for in my practice. One of Sarah's amazing ministries in life was her ability to point to our God as a source of profound joy, strength, and hope, even as her body crumbled before our eyes.

Romans 8:35-39 says,

> Who will separate us from the love of Christ? Will tribula-
> tion, or distress, or persecution, or famine, or nakedness, or
> peril, or sword?...But in all these things we overwhelmingly
> conquer through Him who loved us. For I am convinced
> that neither death, nor life, nor angels, nor principalities,
> nor things present, nor things to come, nor powers, nor
> height, nor depth, nor any other created thing, will be able
> to separate us from the love of God, which is in Christ Jesus
> our Lord (NASB).

I believe and see every day that we have no hope of achieving
any healing of our physical, emotional, and relational hurts in this
life apart from His grace.

A Faith Reborn

We all have doubts and disappointments with God. We expect healing and miracles and sometimes they show up, but sometimes they
don't. Sometimes they show up in unexpected ways.

Shelly, my son Joshua, you, and I have had our faith shaken. In
our moments of vulnerability, we have all been disappointed by God.
God has not been what you thought He would be and probably has
not done what you thought He should do. But He's God and He gets
to make those decisions.

All in all, emotional and physical crises often lead to spiritual crises. From a crisis, however, we can expect a new life to emerge, a new
faith to be reborn.

Something particular to emotional stress, leading to physical distress, makes one even more reliant and hopeful on God. The span
between hope and disillusionment can be great. However, as you
work through that disappointment and arrive at new understand-
ings, you have the opportunity to have a new, more mature faith—
a faith reborn.

The Path Forward

We have talked about God in this chapter. I haven't been too theological because, frankly, I'm not that theological. I hope, however, I've walked with you through some of the theological questions (and answers) about what many experience when facing severe stress—most presumably, doubt.

The bottom line is God cannot be or ever will be fully understood. If that were possible, we'd be more like God than we are. "Now we see only a reflection as in a mirror; then we shall see face to face. Now I know in part; then I shall know fully, even as I am fully known" (1 Corinthians 13:12).

Let's now continue our journey toward healing by learning how to take responsibility for your health.

ELEVEN

TAKING RESPONSIBILITY FOR YOUR HEALTH

*I believe that the greatest gift you can give to
your family and the world is a healthy you.*

—JOYCE MEYER

I don't want to take responsibility for my health. I really don't. I know that's not the most mature response I could give, but it's the truth.

Even though I know my health is ultimately my responsibility, I want to pawn off that responsibility on doctors and nurses. I want "the medical profession" to take care of me, no matter what happens.

This, of course, is a childish notion. Intellectually I know there is not a doctor on the planet who cares for my well-being as much as I care for my well-being. But having been indoctrinated into believing doctors and the medical profession are all powerful and all knowing, contrasted with my feeble understanding of what is happening within me and to me, I defer to the doctor every time.

Perhaps you can relate. This chapter is a slap-in-the-face reality check to remind you and me that our well-being is ultimately up to us. Any understanding or action contrary to this will be incredibly disappointing.

M. Deity

As a child I distinctly remember being taken to the doctor. I was always happy to go to the doctor because it meant I would miss school, spend time with my mom, and probably get some kind of treat for being brave.

Dr. August Zoet was, from my youthful perspective, a big, friendly man, with large, black glasses, who knew everything. Why else would my mother take me to see him when I wasn't feeling well?

He was, in a very real way, the next thing to God. In fact, if it's possible, he was actually bigger than God. God, after all, apparently wasn't able to treat my bronchitis, while Dr. Zoet could. God didn't know what to do when I contracted the measles, but Dr. Zoet took immediate action.

My youthful perspective of comparing doctors to God was only amplified over the years. While I had successfully navigated the mumps and measles in my early years, at 17 years old I had a sudden, and quite traumatic, asthmatic episode. With all due respect to God, it was Dr. J. David Hughes who hospitalized me and doctored me back to health.

When another severe asthmatic episode struck, I was a financially destitute 20-year-old college student at the University of Washington. It was a doctor from a free medical clinic, whose name I've regretfully forgotten, who spent untold hours with me, teaching me how to percuss my chest and manage the perils of asthma. I've never forgotten his kindness and understanding as I suffered from this debilitating condition.

Adding to his larger-than-life persona, this doctor actually made house calls. He cared enough to visit me at home and teach me skills to mitigate the frightening impact of asthma. Loss of breath can be terrifying, but not so much when the doctor is in the house.

I have not stopped bestowing upon doctors an inordinate amount of praise and respect—too much, undoubtedly. I have never been seriously disappointed by the medical profession and have always found them to be gracious and generous with advice, medicine, and expert help.

Are there doctors who perform badly? Undoubtedly. Do some take advantage of their power, wealth, and position? Yes. As you have struggled with your health, your experience may be far less favorable than mine. You may have encountered an egotistical physician who really epitomized the pejorative title, "M. Deity," and for that I am sorry. Doctors are not God, and sooner or later we all come to that realization.

The Passive Approach

My perspective may also be colored by my passive nature. I tend to put all my trust in doctors, dentists, lawyers, and other professionals. I am far too naive, and I know it. Still, I'm passive.

Many others are passive as well. Historically most consumers have been passive when it comes to medical care. Perhaps you, too, have taken a passive approach to yours. Perhaps you have sat back, placing your total care into the hands of your physician.

The days of the family doctor coming to your home are gone. Gone also are the days of having one doctor who will follow you through the course of your healthcare needs. The healthcare system has, as we have all experienced, changed. You are more likely to see multiple clinicians, in multiple settings.

With these changes we need to view the patient's role as a job, and then design that job to best drive health outcomes.

Healthcare has changed for all of us over the past 20 years. Leave it to those seeking greater profits—corporations—to influence our approach to healthcare. Provider reimbursements are now more directly tied to outcomes, and outcomes are tied to proficiencies—whether tests and interventions really do what they are expected to do and truly help the patient. Because of these changes we are more likely to seek care outside the walls of the traditional clinic, through urgent care centers, virtual consults, or alternative therapies.

Len Schlesinger and John Fox, in their article "Giving Patients an Active Role in Their Healthcare," say,

> What's needed is a fundamental redesign of the patient's role—from that of a passive recipient of care to an active participant charged with defined responsibilities, equipped to dispatch them, and accountable for the results.[1]

While you may resist taking a more active approach to your care, the evidence demonstrates that patients who are more actively involved in their healthcare have better health outcomes and spend less money in the process.

Your Health Quiz

There are basically two approaches to maintaining or restoring your health and wellness: Passive and active. I already revealed that my approach has always been passive, though that may soon change. Stay tuned.

Take a moment to take a brief quiz about your approach to healthcare. Where do you fit in? Passive or active? Get your pencil ready and begin.

Passive Healthcare

1. Do you complain and whine about what ails you but resist going to the doctor?

2. Are you reactive in your medical care, going to the doctor only after you've experienced a significant amount of pain?

3. Do you avoid taking the doctor's suggestions for ongoing, optimal healthcare?

4. Do you avoid participating in optimal healthcare practices you know would be good for you such as exercise, proper nutrition, work-life balance, sleep, and interpersonal care?

5. Do you engage in practices such as smoking, excessive eating, excessive alcohol use, or nonprescription drug use that you know to be detrimental to your health?

Active Healthcare

1. Are you proactive when it comes to healthcare, getting regular physicals, colon screens, and blood work?

2. Do you go to the doctor within an appropriate period of time after experiencing distress?

3. Do you follow your doctor's orders for you?

4. Do you participate in a wide variety of optimal healthcare practices in order to be as healthy as possible?

5. Do you avoid unhealthy practices such as smoking, excessive eating, excessive alcohol use, or nonprescription drug use that you know to be detrimental to your health?

Okay. Where do you fall? Passive or active? What jumped out at you as you answered the above questions? Be honest, because you cannot make changes if you are not honest with yourself.

If you're like most people, you complain and then soldier through the pain, hoping it will go away. Or, at the other extreme, you shop for a doctor who tells you exactly what you want to hear. Neither extreme is ideal. We must take proper care of ourselves and find healthcare providers who are sympathetic to our situation and our medical orientation. Then work together to achieve agreed-upon goals.

Judith

Judith is a 40-year-old mother of three who is 30 pounds overweight and feels horrible. She is married to a workaholic attorney who is intense and unforgiving. She is miserable in her toxic marriage and came to see me to consider her options.

"Coming here was my idea," she proclaimed. "Herb won't come to counseling. He says he's tried counseling in the past and it hasn't done any good."

"Is that true?" I asked.

"Sort of. We have gone to a couple of marriage counselors for three or four visits each time," Judith said. "But Herb finds something wrong with each one. He really doesn't want to be confronted, so when they step on his toes in the slightest, he's out of there."

"So, tell me some more about your marriage," I said.

"It's terrible," she said. "I busy myself with my job and the kids and try to forget how unhappy I am. Herb is a busy attorney with no time to really invest in our marriage. Anytime I ask for more of his attention he gets angry. Now I just leave the angry bear alone."

"How does he feel about the marriage?" I asked.

"I don't have a clue," she said. "We avoid each other. I've wondered if he's having an affair, but I don't really think so. His lover is the courtroom. That's where he gets all of his accolades. I guess I do the same with my job. I'm respected there."

"What about the kids?" I asked.

"They are my joy," she said. "I'm involved in all their sports. They help take my mind off my unhappy marriage. They notice their dad and I never do anything together. They notice he is critical of me. I've gotten to the point where I snap back. They notice that too."

"What do you want to do about your situation?" I asked.

"Great question," she said. "I know I've got to do something. I'm gaining more and more weight. I'm more tired than I've ever been. My cholesterol is skyrocketing and my blood pressure is out of control. I know it's stress. But I don't know where to begin."

"I think the place to begin is for us to do a marriage evaluation," I said.

"What is that?" she asked.

"I will take a thorough marriage history from you and do the same with Herb. Then we'll get together and determine a direction for you folks."

"But he won't come," she said.

"Are you really sure about that?" I said. "Many times when women are consistent and persistent the men come in. When they realize that you mean business, assuming you do, and talk about 'the elephant in the room' regarding your marriage unhappiness, they will show up."

"Well," she said slowly, "I guess it's worth a try."

We spent the next few weeks taking a detailed history of her marriage. It was painful for her to be honest with herself about her emotional and marital pain. She explored how she had been impacted by her husband's anger, how she had become discouraged over the years, and had become passive in not only her approach to her marriage but her approach to her healthcare as well. The solutions lay in her taking an active interest in both.

Changing Directions

Crises are times of change and often bring a change of direction. It is time for Judith to change directions. She must take a much more active role in the wellness of her marriage as well as her physical and spiritual wellness. Her passivity is literally killing her.

Judith's decision to come and see me was a powerful one. Change begins as we consider change. Her presence at her sessions indicated she has already contemplated more significant change. She has already decided the way she is living is not satisfying and a better life can be hers with some work.

About 20 years ago, two alcoholism researchers, Carlo C. DiClemente and J.O. Prochaska, released a five-stage model of change to help professionals understand their clients' issues with addiction. Using their model can help you honestly assess and understand where you are in the change process, helping you to gain greater influence over the choices you make. Here are the stages of change:

1. *Precontemplation.* In this stage individuals are not even thinking about changing their behavior. They may not see it as a problem and are in denial about the severity of their condition.

2. *Contemplation.* In this stage individuals consider the possibility they have a problem and consider the possibility of change. However, at this point individuals are typically highly ambivalent. Contemplation is not a commitment to change.

3. *Determination.* In this stage individuals are committed to action. They have stepped off the fence and begin to make concrete plans for change. While all their ambivalence has not been resolved, they are moving in the right direction.

4. *Action.* In this stage individuals take action. Whatever the focus of their concern, they now put into motion some concrete steps. They have begun to change.

5. *Maintenance.* Having begun the change process, success now depends on making their actions a regular part of their life. The beginning change process must become

a habit, integrated into their life, for them to find true
success.

6. *Termination.* In this stage individuals have no desire to
   return to their unhealthy behavior and are sure they will
   not slide backwards. This stage, incidentally, is rarely
   reached.[2]

Judith is clearly ready for change. She has moved through the contemplation stage and is now taking action. She has not yet reached a point
where change is automatic or habitual, but she is on her way to healing.

Momentum

Judith has something very strong going for her, something perhaps you recognize in yourself: *Momentum.* Momentum is a powerful concept.

What do I mean by momentum? Momentum is energy—our accel-
erator as we move through life. When we contemplate making changes
and consider taking more responsibility for our health and emotional
well-being, momentum is what carries us from point A to point B. Uti-
lizing momentum, after we've determined where we want to go, we
have the go-power to get us to that place we've envisioned.

Notice the momentum Judith has already exerted. She has done
a great deal of reflecting on her situation. That takes effort and focus.
She has read books, watched videos, and sought counseling. That takes
additional effort and focus. She had to have momentum to carry her
forward. She has moved through several stages of change. That also
takes momentum. So when you think about it, Judith is already well
on her way to her goal of having a healthy relationship and healthy life.

In his article "The Power of Momentum," Michael Thomas Sunnarborg writes,

> The mind is powerful and our thoughts have energy. When
> we focus on a thought and give it our attention, that energy
> affects what we say and do in response. Once a thought
> gets enough attention, it begins to gather momentum.[3]

Still, Judith wants more. Who can blame her? She wants to either change the way she relates to her husband or end their destructive relationship. That is a valid goal. She wants to be healthier, both emotionally and physically. These are also worthwhile goals. Will this be enough?

When we remind ourselves that momentum is motion and progress toward a goal, she is doing fairly well. However, she could do better. Perhaps you find yourself in a similar mind-set: You are moving in a positive direction but want more. What can you do to increase your momentum and forward movement?

1. *Clarify your goals.* Goals must have clarity to be effective. You must determine what it is exactly that you want. Sort wants from needs, desires from necessities.

2. *Seek a health coach.* We all need help to clarify our goals, where we want to go, and the best approach to get there. A health coach can help you become clearer and more determined in your approach.

3. *Specify your goals.* Make your goals very specific. For example, you may decide to join a women's support group. You may decide to read certain books and journal. You may add exercise and other health goals to your list.

4. *Target date your goals.* Goals must have target dates if you are going to reach them. Nonspecific target dates end up never being reached. Get a calendar and check off the dates as you work toward your goals, aiming for your target end date.

5. *Evaluate your goals.* Goals must be evaluated to determine if more time is needed, if the goals need to be changed or modified, or if they are hitting the mark. Honestly appraise your actions to see if they fit with your overall purpose.

6. *Revise your goals.* After evaluating your goals, revise them accordingly. Sit down with a trusted friend or professional and determine if your goals are still relevant and appropriate or if they need to be changed and revised.

7. *Champion your goals.* As you achieve your goals, notice the excitement that comes from these accomplishments. Pat yourself on the back and endeavor to keep the chain of events moving forward. Soon your positive actions will become habits.

As you move through these steps you will feel even more power, more momentum. You won't want to stop or lose the positive energy derived from achieving goals.

Tolerating Setbacks

There is no perfect plan. While I want you to make solid plans and enjoy positive momentum, you must also be prepared for setbacks.

We all know that any journey is speckled with victories and losses, thrills and heartache. We know this intellectually, and yet every disappointment can be our reason for not getting back into the game.

One example of rising above one's circumstances comes to mind. Rocky is a hero of mine. How can you not pull for that guy? In the 2006 movie *Rocky Balboa*, we see a scene where Rocky's son is not thrilled about his father going back into the ring. He has seen his father win some and lose some, and the losses have been excruciating. Still, Rocky is determined to try again.

Looking at his son, Rocky says this: "It ain't about how hard you hit. It's about how hard you can get hit and keep moving forward. How much you can take and keep moving forward. That's how winning is done!"

He is saying that we all face adversity. We all have times of failure. We can't win all the time. We can't be good at everything. But if a goal is important enough to us, we must dig deep inside us for that inner fortitude to keep going, to get up and fight again.

We all have the power to choose to get up and persevere.

The Power of Choice

Much distress in life comes from the perception that we have no choice in a matter. Think about it. When you feel powerless you feel more discouraged.

Recently my wife and I had to replace both our washer and dryer. This came just a short time after we had to put our car in the shop for the second time.

I had a case of the blues.

Why are all these things breaking down? I asked myself. *Why is this happening to me?*

Now you may be smiling at my story for several reasons. Perhaps you've been there. Or perhaps you're thinking, *I wish that were all I had to worry about.* You might be thinking it is pretty silly of me to spend negative energy on something largely outside of my control.

The truth is, things break down. Cars, home appliances, and things in general take energy and will undoubtedly be sources of frustration. But it is also true that while I have little control over whether we replace our washer and dryer—we want the comfort of having the freedom of washing our clothes at home—we *do* have a choice in many other areas of our lives.

We are all given a large amount of power, and that power comes in the form of choice. We *are* able to choose how active to be in our healthcare. We *are* able to choose how hard we work to attain our goals. We *are* able to have a direct impact on lessening the stress in our lives and in some ways the quality of our relationships.

Unfortunately, many people fail to *learn* to utilize the power they have to make choices. They settle into a passive approach to life and sometimes worse—a kind of helplessness that is unnecessary.

Dr. Martin Seligman discovered a powerful concept called *learned helplessness* in which a person who has experienced significant trauma becomes unable or unwilling to avoid subsequent traumatic experiences even if those experiences are escapable. The person perceives they have no control or choice over their world, when in fact they do, and they act according to their perception.

Fortunately, Dr. Seligman also discovered a "cure" for this helplessness—*learned optimism.* Seligman found that we are all capable of cultivating positive feelings such as joy and happiness, as well as noticing our power of choice and the impact that has on our lives.[4]

A Path to Better Health

You *do* have choices, and the choices you make impact how you will feel. In a very real sense, you choose how happy and healthy you will be. This comes through the power of choice.

According to Lubna Najjar, in her article "The Power of Choice," the average working adult makes about 12 decisions before 9:00 a.m. She reports that an adult makes 70-plus decisions a day.[5]

Many of these decisions, of course, aren't really decisions. I don't consciously decide to roll out of bed on my right side or not, to snooze or not when my alarm goes off. I don't stop and decide whether or not to take my blood pressure medicine. These decisions are habitual.

But as it pertains to my mental and relational health, I have decided to promptly admit when I'm wrong. Instead of making excuses, I want to be a person who is capable of owning up to wrongdoing and make it right with the offended person.

I've decided to take better care of my health. I want to be proactive and make doctor's appointments to stay on top of my health to the best of my abilities.

What about you? What decisions do you need to make to optimize your health and well-being? How can you take a more active interest in how you feel on a day-to-day basis?

From a Physician: Dr. Tyson Hawkins, Internist

The first thing that comes to mind when I think of active versus passive medical care is preventative medicine. The first example that comes to mind is the "annual exam," but there are certainly other forms of preventative healthcare as well. My patients frequently ask me whether or not I recommend they come back annually for a "physical." The reason I put quotes around these two concepts is because my answer differs depending on the patient. I prefer the focus of the visit not be on the physical exam itself, but a comprehensive review of the patient's current medical status and ways to prevent future disease. A part of that is the exam itself, but there is so much more.

I *do* recommend preventative medical visits, to be sure. The frequency and complexity of those visits differs drastically depending on the age and overall health of my patient. You should not be surprised to hear that most physicians do not feel an annual exam is necessary in a healthy 22-year-old. Medicare, however, recommends an annual visit for all patients over the age of 65. The content of those visits is very different from that of a visit with a healthy 22-year-old; the physical examination portion is one of the few similarities.

I love to see patients engaged in their healthcare and scheduling these types of visits. While I question the utility of some of our traditions (annual labs for example), I do not question the benefit of having an actively engaged patient. I consider the annual visit to be an opportunity to intervene before things get out of hand. Cancer screening is an obvious example, but developing a healthy and trusting relationship with a patient is also a vital component of these visits. Often the visits are a combination of minor but nagging complaints in addition to basic health screening, including a blood pressure evaluation, weight check, depression screening, and alcohol and tobacco screening. Research has shown limited usefulness to the "annual exam" in regard to improved health outcomes, yet I am unaware of a physician who does not perform them. While I do not believe their usefulness lies in an annual examination of lab work and testing, I do believe there are more subtle benefits.

I can't count the number of times I have seen a patient come in under the premise of an annual physical only to divulge that they have been suffering for quite some time with a variety of potentially serious maladies. When asked what really prompted their visit, they admit they are worried about something. While those fears are often unwarranted, that is not always the case.

Sandra is a 62-year-old woman who recently presented for an annual preventative visit. I had not seen her in more than five years.

She had historically been quite healthy and did not take any prescription medications on a regular basis. Although she had come for "a checkup," she was concerned. She had become increasingly short of breath for the past several months and was complaining of constipation and abdominal fullness. She was not urgently concerned, which is why she chose to wait for a preventative visit to discuss her concerns. The outcome of her tests showed metastatic ovarian cancer with fluid filling her abdomen and surrounding her lungs.

I do not know if regular preventative examinations would have found her cancer more quickly or if she would have even mentioned her symptoms sooner, but I can't help but wonder. I wonder if she had been more engaged in her healthcare and had a good rapport with her physician if she might have come in sooner to be evaluated. If she had taken an active rather than passive approach, could her cancer have been diagnosed earlier?

The US Preventative Task Force (USPTF) has very specific recommendations regarding screening, and this is what guides most recommendations given by your doctor. These recommendations are based on clinical research showing proven benefits to certain examinations for certain populations. There is not a one-size-fits-all approach to preventative care, and I would encourage you to talk with your healthcare provider regarding what examinations (if any) are appropriate for you at this time. Become an active participant in your care!

Collaborative Medicine

You want to feel better. Your marriage and other relationships are challenging, and this has impacted your health and well-being.

Things won't automatically improve. You must take your relationships, health, and well-being into your control and make some changes.

It is common for patients who come to see me or my sons to expect miracles. Let's face it. This passive approach is wishful thinking at best, magical thinking at worst. Hoping, wishing, complaining, and even praying won't get you to where you want to go.

You must cooperate with several people to get where you want to go.

First, you must cooperate with your physician or medical care-givers. You must work hand in hand with those to whom you've entrusted your care. You must communicate with them, cooperate with them, and collaborate with them. If they are doing their job, they will give you guidance and suggestions on how to become healthier; follow them.

Second, you must cooperate with your counselor. A good counselor will also give you clear, wise guidance on what needs to change to help you gain mastery over your life. You must communicate your desired goals to them, cooperate with them, and collaborate with them. Counseling should be an exciting experience. You should feel encouraged, challenged, and even pushed a bit. Work with them to make it a positive experience.

Finally, you must coordinate with these professionals. It may be that you and your counselor need to confer with your physician. It may be that you need to make sure everyone is on the same page, working toward the same goals. Again, communication is key.

"Plans fail for lack of counsel, but with many advisers they succeed" (Proverbs 15:22).

The Path Forward

In this chapter you've learned that you are ultimately responsible for your care. While you can seek out skilled professionals and learn which friends and family are really there for you, it's ultimately your responsibility to create a path of healing.

It's equally important to bear in mind that no matter your circumstances, you must continue forward on your path. Looking back will help you reflect, grieve, and put things in perspective. But it's important to keep moving forward.

Let's now continue our journey and completion of this book with a discussion about ultimate healing.

TWELVE

ULTIMATE HEALING

Take the first step in faith. You don't
have to see the whole staircase.
Just take the first step.

—DR. MARTIN LUTHER KING JR.

My sons and I, a surgeon, an internist, and a psychologist, have
discussed in this book how we are mind, body, and spirit—all
parts of a miraculous whole, coming together to form who we are.
We've looked at our mind-body connection, how our bodies impact
our minds and our minds impact our bodies. We've reviewed how our
bodies record what is happening to us.

Then we've considered how marriage, and all our relationships,
impact us, sometimes for good and sometimes to our detriment. Too
often we find ourselves coping with problematic and even toxic relationships, and again, our bodies record the events.

We have looked at the impact of stress on the body, from everyday
stress to complex post-traumatic stress disorder. We shared aspects of
stress not commonly understood or addressed.

We looked at some of the ways people cope with stress and encouraged you to delve deeply into your life to see if you might be coping in
unhealthy ways.

We introduced the concept of "emotional hangovers," those dreaded
and exhausting episodes after particularly difficult encounters with a
mate. We spoke about anger—the anger that fuels everything—and
explored not only the emotional fuel that permeates anger but the
impact of anger on you and your relationships.

Then we moved on to discuss feeling lost and alone and the incredible importance of finding support and community. That community often includes church; and we explored how many of us feel let down by friends, family, the church, and ultimately God.

Finally, we began exploring healing and taking responsibility for our health. As we come to the end of this book, I leave you with one last challenge: To rethink how you conceptualize your health and healing—something we call "ultimate healing."

A New View of Healing

Ultimate healing means taking responsibility for your life and your healing. As you embrace this power—the power of choices about your life—our hope is you feel empowered, perhaps even excited about fully owning your life and well-being.

Your mind is the place to begin the ultimate healing of your body. How you view your life, your body, and your future will determine in large part how you feel.

Navigating through this book, you've taken an inventory of your health. You've examined, close up, whether you are passive or active in your healthcare. We want you to look in the mirror, embrace who you are, and get excited about who you want to become, one small step at a time.

What does ultimate healing look like for you? What would be different if you felt better? What has happened in your life to bring you to where you are today, and what are the barriers keeping you from being "the perfect you"?

One of the most common barriers to emotional and physical well-being is having too narrow a view of healing. It is tempting to think in black-and-white terms—sickness or health, right or wrong, good or bad. Our brains love that stuff. Our brains love patterns. Similarities. This is why we easily get stuck in a rut when it comes to our thinking. It's easy to keep thinking the same thoughts, believing the same beliefs, and doing the same things.

But life, health, and a new view of healing are not that simple. They are far more complex, a kaleidoscope of thoughts and feelings. It's no wonder we have trouble sorting out our thoughts and feelings with their complexities.

What if we simplified matters, accepting our life where we are and leaning forward? What if we stopped fighting what is happening to us and focused on the next small step in front of us? What if we attempted to have a new view of healing?

A new view of healing must examine expectations. When we expect to feel healthy and we don't, we feel stress. When we expect to have relationships that work perfectly and they don't, we feel stress. When we expect life to flow easily and smoothly and it doesn't, we feel stress. Then, feeling ongoing stress, our bodies record the process.

Nothing could be more complex than the topic of stress, health, and healing. What is healing? Is it the absence of pain? Is it when we are completely free from any disease process? Is it about never feeling any stress?

We must learn to think about healing in a new way. Ultimate healing is where we join with ourselves and God to love our body, our life, and perhaps even our relationships in a new way.

Another View of Stress

Ultimate healing is living in such a way that you are in tune with your body, your life, and your relationships, and you engage dynamically with them so as to live fully.

We have spent a great deal of time exploring stress and its debilitating impact. But we have yet another view to offer you.

We cannot avoid stress, nor would we really want to. Stress can be described as strings on a guitar—too tight and they break; too loose and they lose their function. Considering this, totally eliminating all stress from your life will not necessarily bring you perfect health.

Stress and tension, then, can be viewed in the same way we view our emotions, as welcome guests sent to give us important messages. Again, using the image of the guitar strings, if we have too little tension we become bored. If we have too much tension, we feel anxious and out of sorts.

Ultimate healing is about listening keenly to our bodies to determine if we are in sync with ourselves. Are we listening to our emotions, our bodies, and all the signals that will help us stay "tuned up"?

An Odd Story

It is an odd story.

The apostle John tells of a man who had been sick for 38 years, lying with "a great multitude" of sick people by the pool of Bethesda waiting for the angel of the Lord to stir the waters so he could be healed.

This is a long time to be sick, to be sure. This man had the hope of being the first person to step into the pool when the angel appeared so he could be healed.

> When Jesus saw him lying there, *and knew that he already had been in that condition a long time,* He said to him, "Do you want to be made well?"
>
> The sick man answered Him, "Sir, I have no man to put me into the pool when the water is stirred up; but while I am coming, another steps down before me."
>
> Jesus said to him, "Rise, take up your bed and walk." And immediately the man was made well, took up his bed, and walked (John 5:6-9 NKJV, emphasis added).

This is an odd story. He had 38 years to get himself into that pool. Why couldn't he do it?

Why did Jesus ask if he wanted to be made well? Why, when Jesus asks him, does he not scream, "Yes, of course I want to be made whole! Will You please, please help me?"

I have several thoughts on this. I wonder if the man had grown accustomed to being sick. It is quite natural, after a significant period of time, to take on certain roles. I wonder if this man assumed the role of a sick, debilitated person experiencing a severe case of inertia.

I also wonder if he had developed secondary gains from being sick. Did he complain often about his plight? He certainly associated with other sick people who were perhaps faring no better than he at getting into that pool and getting well. Was he recognized as "that guy who's been here for 38 years"?

What is perhaps most amazing about this story is that Jesus was not distracted by the man's lack of initiative or lack of friends or the possibility that he has grown complacent about being sick. Jesus simply wanted to know if the man, *in his innermost being, really wanted to be healed,* or whether he was content staying where he was.

The true test comes next. Jesus said, "Rise up," the man obeyed, and he was forever healed. The man has apparently gone through the stages of change, is willing to take action, does so, and experiences healing.

Ultimate healing includes giving up any vestiges of being defined by your sickness and instead embracing healing and health. Ultimate healing is about looking at healing in a new way.

Identification: Patient

Being sick can become an identity. One can feel identified by what is happening to their body.

You may resist being honest with yourself about this. Few admit to identifying with the role of being a patient, with being chronically ill. But pain, disease, stress, and dissatisfaction can begin to define you.

This is often a subtle process. After being diagnosed with asthma, it became second nature for me to carry my inhaler with me. I still rarely leave home without it. For years I compromised my lifestyle because I didn't want to have an exercise-induced asthma attack.

Have you grown accustomed to not feeling well? Has it become second nature to think of yourself as sick as opposed to happy and healthy? Can you see what I mean?

Not identifying with our sickness is a lot easier said than done. As I've shared, I've been an asthmatic for more than 40 years. I'm always aware of my asthma, even when it's not particularly bothering me.

As the years have passed and my symptoms have lessened, I've expanded my view of myself from being an asthmatic to being healthy. Although my symptoms have abated, giving up the role of patient has been as much mental as physical. You may not be at that place yet. After experiencing chronic relationship stress and the natural consequences to your health, letting go of seeing yourself as sick may be a challenge.

Doubts and Secondary Gains

Being sick is a frightening thing. To have a brief cold or spate of flu is one thing; to be chronically ill is quite another. To feel exhausted from chronic stress is stressful, not to mention the emotional challenges leading to that stress.

Why did I come down with asthma at age 16? Doctors scratched their heads and wondered if there was a psychological component to my illness. My older sister, Sharon, had just left home. Did I miss her? Was being "sick" and dependent a more comfortable role?

You know about these doubts. You know about doctors and friends questioning you. "Is this all in your head?" "Do you really want to be healed?" You have considered this question hundreds of times.

Ultimate healing means examining our doubts and fears about healing. Let's be honest. We know people question our real motivations. We know there are those who believe we would rather be sick than well. On certain days, you may give in to these doubts. You may, at times, give up the fight to get better.

Still, we must be mindful and remain steadfast about our wellbeing and choose health. We can achieve healing.

A New Identity

Achieving ultimate healing means looking at ourselves and our situations in an entirely different way. While the man at the pool of Bethesda can be criticized for not being resourceful enough to get into the pool, *for 38 years he did show up*—and the result was the opportunity to say, "Yes, I am here, and I want to be healed."

That's pretty incredible. He showed up. He was there at the pool, day after day, year after year. And, guess what; he showed up on the day Jesus showed up.

And he followed the doctor's orders: "Rise up and walk." He had to have had doubts about that prescription for healing. He had to have wondered, *Are you kidding me? Rise up? That's it?*

You could say the man at the pool was involved in his healing long before that incredible day of ultimate healing. He showed up, day after day, and thereby placed himself in a position to be healed. He had prepared his heart and mind for healing. He was ready for a miracle.

Ultimate healing is a process, not a condition. Ultimate healing is preparing to be healed, preparing to have a new identity beyond your current circumstances. Ultimate healing is healing that comes when we realize we are going to put one foot in front of the other, take the next best step, and keep reaching.

Think about this. Our new identity doesn't occur when we are healed, *if we are healed.* Our new identity begins when we are changed from the inside out. It begins when we see our Self as loved and lovely no matter what is happening in our physical body. We love ourselves enough to really pursue healing—seeking the stirring of the waters, so to speak—and to listen to what God might be saying to us.

Prayer for Healing

We all want to feel better, seeking a return to healthy functioning. No amount of secondary gain, sympathy, compassion, or anything else compares with feeling healthy. You know what I mean. You know that one good day free from pain or exhaustion is worth anything. You know a day free from the psychological distress of a troubled relationship is worth everything.

So you want healing. You long for healing. You pray for healing.

In the past five years I've prayed for healing for my mother, then my father, and finally my sister. They all died.

What has that done to my faith and my belief in healing? Not much, honestly. I still believe in praying for healing, but I know healing may look different than what I want and hope for at the moment. Additionally, my prayers aren't just for healing—they're for so much more, such as peace and acceptance.

My narrow views of what should and should not happen if I have faith have changed. The mystery of God and how God works has widened and deepened. Perhaps it is the same for you.

Embracing a New View of Healing

I'm learning, as I get older, that my view of healing needs to be expanded. My old view of "If I have enough faith I will be healed" has given way to a broader definition of healing.

I can have plenty of faith, be very connected to God, and not be fully physically healed. I have to create space in my faith to allow for bad things to happen. I have to widen my thinking to include different perspectives on healing and health.

My client Katherine taught me so much about healing and a healthy attitude toward stress and sickness. She epitomized this new view of healing. Private and proud, she was at first reluctant to talk about her health.

"My health doesn't define me," she said strongly. "My healthy lifestyle does. I don't decide if it's a good or bad day depending on how I feel. I'm going to look for the blessings in the day and be grateful for another day no matter what happens."

I was skeptical.

"My fibromyalgia is so bad some days that I don't want to get out of bed. But I make myself. I do the things I know will make me feel better. I have completely altered my lifestyle, from the way I work, the food I eat, the exercises I do, and it all makes a difference. Not one thing works completely. All the pieces fit together; and when they do, I'm more likely to have a better day than if I skip any part."

"Tell me what you do that helps, and what hurts?" I asked.

"It has taken me a long time to embrace a new view of healing," she said. "First, I figured out that I alone am responsible for my health. Doctors and health practitioners can help, but ultimately healing is my responsibility."

She paused.

"My husband is still difficult and our marriage is not what I want it to be. But I'm working on improving my relationship with him and not being nearly as affected by things he does or doesn't do.

"There are certain exercises that help me feel better," she added. "Pushing myself is a fine balance. I can't push myself too little or too much. Food is the same. Certain foods make me feel groggy and others enliven me. I'm careful to listen to my body when it comes to food."

"Do you have really bad days?" I asked.

"Yes," she said, "but I don't label them 'bad days.' They are just 'days.' I can usually figure out what triggered a better or worse day. So, again, much is within my control."

Looking at me she smiled and said, "Attitude is everything. I want to encourage everyone to be as healthy as they can be and be grateful for this one body they've been given. My prayers are filled with gratitude for opportunities to seek changes in my life. It's all a gift."

A New, Mindful Lifestyle

When we make the decision to change, having gone through the phases of resisting change, considering change, planning for change, and then actually implementing change, our lives do change.

Ultimate and total healing is not about our bodies fully responding to the "medicine" and recovering in every way; ultimate healing is orienting ourselves to a new lifestyle. Having a new attitude, new habits, and new lifestyle alter how we view life.

Perhaps the words that best define Katherine's lifestyle are *mindful living*. Rather than pushing herself to accomplish more, as if she were a machine, she walks through her day very aware of what she is doing and how she is doing it. She takes life one step at a time, being grateful for every good thing that comes her way.

What do I mean by mindful living? I mean being open and curious about all that is happening in your world. I mean not making judgments about whether your experience is good or bad but rather having compassion for yourself and others.

This also means seeking God in everyday experiences. Living with compassionate attention allows us to focus on what is good about our lives, cultivating clarity, insight, love, and joy. These practices reduce our anxiety and stress and allow us to face our legitimate struggles with increased grace.

Scripture teaches us that we will all face tribulation, and these trials can be incredible teachers.

Not only so, but we also glory in our sufferings, because we know that suffering produces perseverance; perseverance, character; and character, hope. And hope does not put us to shame, because God's love has been poured out into our hearts through the Holy Spirit, who has been given to us (Romans 5:3-5).

There it is. It is our attitude toward our struggles that is telling and instructive. It is our reaction to challenges that creates suffering or peace. We realize we cannot fully control events, but we can choose our attitude in any given set of circumstances. We can embrace God's love, poured into our hearts. We can learn from every ounce of stress that comes our way.

Does this feel like a radical shift? It is hard to overemphasize the importance of this concept. It is our attitude that brings suffering, not the circumstances. It is the way we approach our problems that defines us, not the situation.

I have found that the *Big Book* of Alcoholic's Anonymous offers clear guidance on a proper mind-set when I have stress. The *Big Book* offers this wisdom:

> Acceptance is the answer to *all* my problems today. When I am disturbed, it is because I find some person, place or thing or situation—some fact of life—unacceptable to me, and I can find no serenity until I accept that person, place, thing, or situation as exactly the way it is supposed to be at this moment. Nothing, absolutely nothing happens in God's world by mistake. Until I can accept...life on life's terms, I cannot be happy. I need to concentrate not so much on what needs to be changed in the world as on what needs to be changed in me and in my attitudes.[1]

Although the 12 steps were originally designed for alcoholics, they are fitting for all of us. Learning to accept that there is a God bigger than my circumstances who knows more than I will ever know, and that this moment and its circumstances are unfolding just the way they should, helps me to loosen my grip on circumstances and look within to change my attitude and my lifestyle.

Jonathan and Janet

Jonathan and Janet came to see me like most couples—as a last-ditch effort.

"If this doesn't work, we're ready to call it quits," Janet said. "Twenty years is enough time to give to a marriage. I'm not going to spend the next 20 years feeling this unhappy and exhausted."

Jonathan nodded his head.

Jonathan and Janet made it known they had saved to be able to afford this marriage intensive.

"I'm doing this for her," Jonathan said, his muscular build suggesting he was a powerful man. "It's not the way I expected to spend our money, but she's right. We've got to do something. I don't like us both hurting all the time."

"Tell me what you see," I said.

"She has been more depressed than ever," he said. "She has lost her joy for life."

Jonathan and Janet bickered throughout the first session. They needed to move from blaming and shaming to speaking clearly and with compassion. They had to agree on a deeper reason for coming to see me—to find joy in one another once again.

Both were weary of their fighting and had changed their lifestyle to avoid each other. He spent more time at work than necessary while she invested all her time and attention in their two children. Their relationship was now drained of vitality and filled with tension.

I talked to both about how the issues we fight about are not typically the problem, but rather the *way* we talk about issues is a more critical factor.

I asked them the question I pose to all couples coming to the Marriage Recovery Center.

"On a scale of one to ten, with one being 'never,' five being 'sometimes,' and ten being 'always,' how true is this statement: I feel certain that I can go to my mate with anything on my mind and am sure they will listen to me, help me feel at ease, and assist me in finding a solution to my problem."

Both laughed, hinting at their answer.

"Never," Janet blurted out.

"It's supposed to be a score," Jonathan said sarcastically. "Anyway, I agree. Never for me too."

Their abrupt style softened as we began practicing new skills. As with most couples, their first and most important task was to take on a new view of their pain. Instead of holding to their narrow view that their mate was the sole reason for their emotional and physical pain, they had to shift to seeing their part in the problem. They had to find the real reason they had come to see me—to find joy in their marriage again.

This was central to our work—agreeing on why they had traveled to see me. Why had they saved to come? Why had they prepared their hearts for healing? Why were they now ready for change? Because they wanted new life and grace to fill their marriage.

They needed to embrace joining together to become part of the solution. They had accomplished other huge goals in their lives. Now they needed to come together to find purpose and meaning in healing their marriage, much as you must find purpose and meaning in your healing journey.

"We're in this together, and we can figure this out," I taught again and again. "We can ignore our pain, push it away, and blame our mate for it, but ultimately we must embrace healing. You must see the conflict as representing something that needs to be changed inside of you and between you."

As the saying goes, "Be kind, for everyone is fighting a hard battle."

Slowly they soaked up the little kindnesses of the other. A smile here, and "well done" there. Both appreciated that the other struggled to learn the new skills. Both began to see each other in a new light.

Slowly at first, then more rapidly, hostility gave way to kindness. Distance gave way to connection. Coldness gave way to warmth.

"Do you see what is happening?" I asked. "Can you feel the caring that is just below the surface? Do you see that treating each other with heart creates heart in the other?"

Progress begets progress.

They began to feel empowered. They could impact their own well-being *and* their mate's. They could begin a transformative process. Just as we can be active in our healthcare, we can be active and impactful in our relationship care.

Embracing Health

Individuals and couples can struggle and experience stress but not identify with that struggle. They can detach from their struggle, almost as if the struggle is just a bit separate from them.

They can, instead, identify with their purpose to heal. They can press forward, always seeking health. It's a matter of perspective.

What do you focus on? Do you focus on how much you wish your life were different, or do you focus on how you are taking steps to improve your health?

It's all a matter of perspective.

And what if you have not yet begun your plan to be healthier or to make changes in your marriage like Jonathan and Janet? It's time to start. What Jonathan and Janet did in three days you can do too.

To be healthier takes focus, as a couple or individual. As we close out this book, we want to remind you of what those who embrace health have going for them that the rest of us need to know.

While we cannot definitively determine our health, we can stack the odds in our favor. Here are a few positive steps to take to move you in the right direction.

- *Exercise.* We all know this, right? We feel better when we exercise, lose weight, sleep better, and have more energy. If that weren't enough, studies show those who exercise are sick less often.

- *Wash your hands.* I've got to admit faltering on this one. Studies are clear, however, that the fingertips are home to serious bacteria, and then touching our eyes, nose, and mouth is a quick way to transmit those germs.

- *Have sex.* It's true. Those who have sex on a regular basis have higher levels of an immune system protein called immunoglobulin A (IgA), and this helps keep us healthy.

- *Eat healthy.* We need lots of vegetables and less starchy foods. Fruits and vegetables are full of antioxidants. Add green tea and some probiotics and you have a pretty good plan.

- *Sleep.* No surprise here. Our immune system needs plenty of sleep to stay healthy. While many believe they do fine on six hours of sleep, studies are clear that seven to nine hours of sleep will keep us healthier.

- *Practice mindfulness.* Studies have long noted the benefits of mindfulness, whether this consists of meditation, prayer, or simply short moments of pause when we focus on our breathing.

Whether you are in a position to do all of the above or only a few of them, embrace health and healing. Being your best Self is something you owe yourself and those you love.

What's God Got to Do with It?

Whether you find healing for your marriage and relationships or not, find God. Whether you experience the delightful turnaround that Jonathan and Janet found or not, find God.

As we approach the end of this book, we want you to know that ultimate healing includes finding a satisfying relationship with God. Unique to you and incredibly individual, your relationship to God is completely within your grasp.

Jesus said, "I have come that they may have life, and have it to the full" (John 10:10). Some versions say, "life abundantly."

Abundant life. This is powerful stuff. Who does not want to live life abundantly? We can experience a deep and abiding connection with God, and this brings life.

You can add something intangible to your life no matter how you feel emotionally, physically, or relationally, and this is your relationship to God. You can have an abundant, full life regardless of your relationships.

How is this abundant life possible?

The psalmist says, "In your presence there is fullness of joy; in your right hand are pleasures forevermore" (Psalm 16:11 esv).

Real, ultimate healing comes in our companionship and friendship with God. While we still long to be free from the stress of a troubled marriage or other challenging relationship, and we seek every possible avenue for healing, we embrace our relationship with God.

We never lose sight of the fact that in addition to being physical and emotional beings, we are also spiritual. God is with us and gives us opportunities to change, grow, and heal.

The Path Forward

We have moved together through this book to explore the many faces of stress, the challenges of relationship stress, and the impact it has on us physically. We know God will give us opportunities to be our best selves.

The path forward is a path of love—love for ourselves and compassion for everyone in our world. With a prayer to God and a conviction to be personally accountable for your well-being, plan your next best step.

Looking back has limited value. Pressing forward, into a world filled with possibilities, is the path my sons and I hope you will take. We go with you on your journey, having offered our various skills and insights, hopes and wishes, and a strong belief that you will find your way.

Peace and blessings to you on your journey.

NOTES

Chapter 1—The Mind-Body Connection

1. Clare Kittredge, "The Physical Side of Stress," *Everyday Health*, December 14, 2017, https://www.everydayhealth.com/womens-health/physical-side-of-stress.aspx.

2. Alex Lickerman, "Psychosomatic Symptoms," *Psychology Today*, March 4, 2010, https://www.psychologytoday.com/us/blog/happiness-in-world/201003/psychosomatic-symptoms.

3. Ashley Oerman, "9 Ways Stress Messes with Your Body," *Women's Health*, May 1, 2017, https://www.womenshealthmag.com/health/side-effects-of-stress.

4. Oerman, "9 Ways Stress Messes with Your Body."

5. Matthew Tull, "PTSD and Physical Health," Verywell Mind, February 19, 2017, https://www.verywellmind.com/ptsd-and-physical-health-2797522.

6. American Psychological Association, http://www.sustainable-leaders.com/men-women-differences-stress/.

Chapter 2—Unhealthy Marriage, Unhealthy Body

1. Michael Misja and Chuck Misja, "Thriving Despite a Difficult Marriage," Crosswalk, September 17, 2009, https://www.crosswalk.com/family/marriage/thriving-despite-a-difficult-marriage-11608652.html.

2. Rosemary K.M. Sword and Philip Zimbardo, "Toxic Relationships," *Psychology Today*, August 23, 2013, https://www.psychologytoday.com/us/blog/the-time-cure/201308/toxic-relationships.

Chapter 3—My Lonely, Disappearing Life

1. Julie Axelrod, "The 5 Stages of Grief and Loss," PsychCentral, September 17, 2017, https://psychcentral.com/lib/the-5-stages-of-loss-and-grief/.

2. Bessel van der Kolk, *The Body Keeps the Score* (New York: Penguin Books, 2014), 67.

3. Ibid.

4. Patti Digh, *Life Is a Verb* (Guilford, CT: The Globe Pequot Press, 2008), 140.

5. Julia Cameron, *The Artist's Way* (New York: Penguin, 2001), 163.

6. Van der Kolk, *The Body Keeps the Score*, 100.

Chapter 4—The Struggle for a Self

1. George Simon, "Healing the Fractured Self," Counselling Resource, March 27, 2017, https://counsellingresource.com/features/2017/03/27/healing-fractured-self/.

2. Peter Levine, *In an Unspoken Voice* (Berkeley, CA: North Atlantic Books, 2010), 136-37.

3. David Gommé, "The Only Way to Effectively Contain Stress: New Self-Discovery," Future Dynamics, 2015, https://www.futuredynamics.global/the-fulcrum/way-effectively-contain-stress-new-self-discovery/.

4. Bessel van der Kolk, *The Body Keeps the Score* (New York: Penguin, 2014), 353.

5. William Backus and Marie Chapian, *Telling Yourself the Truth* (Minneapolis, MN: Baker, 1980), 14.

Chapter 5–What You've Never Been Told About Stress

1. "What Is C-PTSD?" Beauty After Bruises, https://www.beautyafterbruises.org/what-is-cptsd/.

2. Ibid.

3. Neel Burton, "Building Confidence and Self-Esteem," *Psychology Today,* May 30, 2012, https://www.psychologytoday.com/us/blog/hide-and-seek/201205/building-confidence-and-self-esteem.

4. Ruth Lanius, Paul A. Frewen, Bethany Brand, "Dissociative Aspects of Posttraumatic Stress Disorder: Epidemiology, Clinical Manifestations, Assessment, and Diagnosis," UpToDate, April 2, 2018, https://www.uptodate.com/contents/dissociative-aspects-of-posttraumatic-stress-disorder-epidemiology-clinical-manifestations-assessment-and-diagnosis#H1288134.

5. Bessel van der Kolk, *The Body Keeps the Score* (New York: Penguin Books, 2014), 249.

Chapter 6–Exhaustion and the Emotional Hangover

1. Scott Peck, *The Road Less Travelled* (New York: Simon & Schuster, 1978), 104, quoted in John Bradshaw, *Healing the Shame that Binds You* (Deerfield Beach, FL: Health Communications, 2005), 29.

2. Traci Pedersen, "Depersonalization," PsychCentral, January 8, 2018, https://psychcentral.com/encyclopedia/depersonalization/.

3. Adele Ryan McDowell, "5 Ways to Deal with an Emotional Hangover," Huffington Post, March 7, 2017, http://www.huffingtonpost.ca/adele-mcdowell/emotional-hangover-cures_b_15198720.html.

Chapter 7–The Anger That Fuels Everything

1. David Hawkins, *The Power of Emotional Decision Making* (Eugene, OR: Harvest House, 2008), 105.

2. Jennice Vilhauer, "Do You Have Toxic Anger Issues and Not Know It?" *Psychology Today,* June 11, 2017, https://www.psychologytoday.com/us/blog/living-forward/201706/do-you-have-toxic-anger-issues-and-not-know-it.

3. Diana Anderson-Tyler, "Anger: A Toxic Emotion that May Be Killing You," Charisma News, January 4, 2014, https://www.charismanews.com/opinion/42272-4-health-dangers-of-anger.

4. Leon F Seltzer, "Anger—How We Transfer Feelings of Guilt, Hurt, and Fear," *Psychology Today,* June 14, 2013, https://www.psychologytoday.com/us/blog/evolution-the-self/201306/anger-how-we-transfer-feelings-guilt-hurt-and-fear.

5. Richard Rohr, *Falling Upward* (San Francisco, CA: Jossey-Bass, 2011), 133.

6. https://www.brainyquote.com/authors/stephen_hawking.

7. Harville Hendrix, *Getting the Love You Want* (New York: Harper, 1988), 174.

8. Hawkins, *The Power of Emotional Decision Making*, 109-10.

9. Terrence Gorski, *Getting Love Right* (New York: Simon & Schuster, 1993), 153.

10. Dan Baker and Cameron Stauth, *What Happy People Know* (New York: St. Martin's Griffin, 2003), 136.

11. Yoichi Chida and Andrew Steptoe, "The Association of Anger and Hostility with Future Coronary Heart Disease," *Journal of the American College of Cardiology* 53, no. 11 (March 2009): 936-46.

12. S.H. Golden, J.E. Williams, D.E. Ford, H.C. Yeh, C.P. Sanford, F.J. Nieto, F.L. Brancati.

"Anger Temperament Is Modestly Associated with the Risk of Type 2 Diabetes Mellitus: The Atherosclerosis Risk in Communities," *Psychoneuroendocrinology* 31, no. 3 (April 2006): 325-32.

13. A. Romero-Martinez, M. Lila, S. Vitoria-Estruch, L. Moya-Albiol, "Imunoglobulin A Levels Mediate the Association Between High Anger Expression and Low Somatic Symptoms in Intimate Partner Violence Perpetrators," *Journal of Interpersonal Violence* 31, no. 4 (February 2016): 732-42.

Chapter 8—Lost, Alone, and Searching for Community

1. Gretchen Rubin, "7 Types of Loneliness (and Why It Matters)," GretchenRubin.com, February 23, 2017, https://gretchenrubin.com/2017/02/7-types-of-loneliness.

2. Shefali Tsabary, "The Power of Validation," DrShefali.com, October 29, 2015, https://drshefali.com/the-power-of-validation/.

3. Karyn Hall, "Understanding the Levels of Validation," PsychCentral, February 5, 2012, https://blogs.psychcentral.com/emotionally-sensitive/2012/02/understanding-the-levels-of-validation/.

4. Henry Cloud, *Changes that Heal* (Grand Rapids: Zondervan, 1992), 65-66.

5. Rosamund Stone Zander and Benjamin Zander, *The Art of Possibility: Transforming Professional and Personal Life* (New York: Penguin, 2000).

6. Charles R. Swindoll, *Dropping Your Guard* (New York: W Publishing Group, 1984).

7. Matthew Sickling, "Are You Wearing a Mask?" SermonCentral, September 7, 2008, https://www.sermoncentral.com/sermons/are-you-wearing-a-mask-matthew-sickling-sermon-on-stress-126589.

8. N.K. Valtorta, M. Kanaan, S. Gilbody, et al., "Loneliness and social isolation as risk factors for coronary heart disease and stroke: systematic review and meta-analysis of longitudinal observational studies," *Heart* 102, no. 13 (July 2016): 1009-16.

9. J. Holt-Lunstad, T.B. Smith, and M. Baker, et al., "Loneliness and Social Isolation as Risk Factors for Mortality: A Meta-Analytic Review," *Perspectives on Psychological Science* 10, no. 2 (March 2015): 227-37.

Chapter 9—Healing Relationships, Mind, and Body

1. Alain de Botton, *The Course of Love* (New York: Simon & Schuster, 2016), 17.

2. Mark Knapp, *Social Intercourse: From Greeting to Goodbye* (New York: Allyn and Bacon, 1978).

3. Belinda Luscombe, "How Marriage May Literally Break Your Heart…Or Keep It Healthy," *Time*, September 8, 2017, http://time.com/4929264/the-real-link-between-marriage-and-heart-attacks/.

4. As quoted in Luscombe, "How Marriage May Literally Break Your Heart."

5. Luscombe, "How Marriage May Literally Break Your Heart."

6. Walter E. Jacobson, "How to Heal Relationships: What's Love and Communication Got to Do With It? Part One," Huffington Post, last updated November 8, 2013, https://www.huffingtonpost.com/walter-e-jacobson-md/relationship-advice_b_3886437.html.

7. Linda Bloom and Charles Bloom, "The Healing Power of Relationships," PsychCentral, December 2, 2013, https://blogs.psychcentral.com/relationship-skills/2013/12/the-healing-power-of-relationships/.

Chapter 10—Disappointment with God

1. Elisabeth K. Corcoran, "Emotional Abuse in Marriage," Just Between Us, http://justbetweenus.org/relationships/marriage-advice/emotional-abuse/.

2. Stephen Arterburn, *Toxic Faith* (Colorado Springs, CO: Waterbrook Press, 1991), 67, 78.

3. Dave Ferguson, "5 Stages of Spiritual Awakening," *Christianity Today,* March 2015, http://www .christianitytoday.com/pastors/2015/march-online-only/5-stages-of-spiritual-awakening.html.

4. Kathleen Norris, *Amazing Grace* (New York: Riverhead Books, 1998), 63.

5. Victor Hugo, "M. Madeleine in Mourning." *Les Miserables*, chapter IV.

Chapter 11—Taking Responsibility for Your Health

1. Len Schlesinger and John Fox, "Giving Patients an Active Role in Their Health Care," *Harvard Business Review,* November 21, 2016, https://hbr.org/2016/11/giving-patients-an-active-role -in-their-health-care.

2. Mark S. Gold, "Stages of Change," PsychCentral, February 13, 2006, https://psychcentral.com/ lib/stages-of-change/?all=1.

3. Michael Thomas Sunnarborg, "The Power of Momentum," Huffington Post, June 20, 2016, https://www.huffingtonpost.com/michael-thomas-sunnarborg/the-power-of-momentum_b _10571454.html.

4. Courtney Ackerman, "Learned Helplessness: Seligman's Theory of Depression (+ Cure)," Positive Psychology Program, March 24, 2018, https://positivepsychologyprogram.com/ learned-helplessness-seligman-theory-depression-cure/.

5. Lubna Najjar, "The Power of Choice," Huffington Post, February 14, 2015, https://www.huff ingtonpost.com/lubna-najjar/the-power-of-choice_1_b_6683212.html.

Chapter 12—Ultimate Healing

1. Anonymous, *Alcoholics Anonymous: The Big Book,* Fourth Edition (Alcoholics Anonymous World Services, Inc., 1976), 417.

ABOUT THE AUTHORS

David Hawkins, MA, MBA, MSW, PhD, is a clinical psychologist and director of the Marriage Recovery Center. Since he began his work in 1976, he has helped bring healing to thousands of marriages and individuals. He is passionate about working with couples in crisis and offering them ways to heal their wounds and find their way back to being passionately in love with each other.

Dr. Hawkins is also a speaker and trainer for the American Association of Christian Counselors and writes for Crosswalk.com, CBN.org, and GrowTrac.com. He is a bestselling author of more than 40 books, including *When Pleasing Others Is Hurting You* and *When Loving Him Is Hurting You: Help and Healing for Women Struggling with Narcissistic and Emotional Abuse.*

For the past ten years, Dr. Hawkins and his staff at the Marriage Recovery Center have become leaders in the field of treatment for narcissism and emotional abuse within relationships. They now offer several programs of treatment for those dealing with and suffering from these issues. Dr. Hawkins is also available to speak at events covering topics such as emotional abuse, narcissism, and healing from relationships with these issues.

If you need specialized help in your relationship or would like to have Dr. Hawkins speak at your next event, please contact:

The Marriage Recovery Center
206.219.0145
www.marriagerecoverycenter.com

Tyson Hawkins, MD, is a practicing internal medicine physician living in Bellingham, Washington, with his wife, Jordana, and two boys, Parker and Bekham. He enjoys any and all things outdoors and spending time with his family. When not in the office, he can be found building a treehouse with his boys or camping with his family in the beautiful Northwest.

Joshua Hawkins, MD, is a follower of Christ, husband, father, surgeon, climber, bike rider, skier, fisherman, and general outdoorsman, in that order. He is a practicing general surgeon, with a focus on cancer surgery. He lives in Mount Vernon, Washington.

OTHER BOOKS BY DAVID HAWKINS

Dealing with the CrazyMakers in Your Life

People who live in chaos and shrug off responsibility drive others crazy. Dr. David Hawkins helps those caught up in a disordered person's life to set boundaries, confront the behavior, and find peace.

When Pleasing Others Is Hurting You

Christians who forfeit their God-given calling and identity in order to please others move from servanthood to codependency. How can they get back on track? Hawkins offers a Christian perspective on healthy relationships and the pitfalls of being a people pleaser. 75,000 copies sold.

When Loving Him Is Hurting You

You've fallen in love with a man who's in love with himself—and the emotional pain his behavior causes you is very real. Dr. David Hawkins shares the truths, wisdom, and grace you need to spark change, set boundaries, and experience healing.

To learn more about Harvest House books and
to read sample chapters, visit our website:

www.harvesthousepublishers.com

HARVEST HOUSE PUBLISHERS
EUGENE, OREGON